W9-BYA-980

DEFINING MOMENTS
PROHIBITION

DEFINING MOMENTS
PROHIBITION

Jeff Hill

615 Griswold, Detroit MI 48226

Omnigraphics, Inc.

Kevin Hillstrom, *Series Editor*
Cherie D. Abbey, *Managing Editor*
Barry Puckett, *Librarian*
Liz Barbour, *Permissions Associate*

Matthew P. Barbour, *Senior Vice President*
Kay Gill, *Vice President – Directories*
Kevin Hayes, *Operations Manager*
Leif A. Gruenberg, *Development Manager*
David P. Bianco, *Marketing Director*

Peter E. Ruffner, *Publisher*
Frederick G. Ruffner, *Chairman*

Copyright © 2004 Omnigraphics, Inc.
ISBN 0-7808-0768-5

Library of Congress Cataloging-in-Publication Data

Prohibition / by Jeff Hill.
     p. cm. -- (Defining moments)
   Includes bibliographical references (p.   ) and index.
   ISBN 0-7808-0768-5 (hardcover : alk. paper)
   1. Prohibition--United States--History--20th century. 2.
Prohibition--United States--History--20th century--Sources. I. Hill,
Jeff,
   1962- II. Series.
   HV5089.P746 2004
 > 363.4'1'097309042--dc22

                                                    2004022643

TABLE OF CONTENTS

NARRATIVE OVERVIEW

BIOGRAPHIES

PRIMARY SOURCES

PREFACE

Throughout the course of America's existence, its people, culture, and institutions have been periodically challenged by—and in many cases transformed by—profound historical events. Some of these momentous events, such as women's suffrage, the civil rights movement, and U.S. involvement in World War II, invigorated the nation and strengthened American confidence and capabilities. Others, such as the McCarthy era, the Vietnam War, and Watergate, have prompted troubled assessments and heated debates about the country's core beliefs and character.

Some of these defining moments in American history were years or even decades in the making. The Harlem Renaissance and the New Deal, for example, unfurled over the span of several years, while the American labor movement and the Cold War evolved over the course of decades. Other defining moments, such as the Cuban missile crisis and the terrorist attacks of September 11, 2001, transpired over a matter of days or weeks.

But although significant differences exist among these events in terms of their duration and their place in the timeline of American history, all share the same basic characteristic: they transformed the United States' political, cultural, and social landscape for future generations of Americans.

Taking heed of this fundamental reality, American citizens, schools, and other institutions are increasingly emphasizing the importance of understanding our nation's history. Omnigraphics' *Defining Moments* series was created for the express purpose of meeting this growing appetite for authoritative, useful historical resources. This series, which focuses on the most pivotal events in U.S. history from the 20th century forward, will be of enduring value to anyone interested in learning more about America's past—and in understanding how those historical events continue to reverberate in the 21st century.

Each individual volume of *Defining Moments* provides a valuable resource for readers interested in learning about the most profound events in our nation's history. Each volume is organized into three distinct sections—Narrative Overview, Biographies, and Primary Sources.

- The **Narrative Overview** provides readers with a detailed, factual account of the origins and progression of the "defining moment" being examined. It also explores the event's lasting impact on America's political and cultural landscape.

- The **Biographies** section provides valuable biographical background on leading figures associated with the event in question. Each biography concludes with a list of sources for further information on the profiled individual.

- The **Primary Sources** section collects a wide variety of pertinent primary source materials from the era under discussion, including official documents, papers and resolutions, letters, oral histories, memoirs, editorials, and other important works.

Individually, each of these sections is a rich resource for users. Together, they comprise an authoritative, balanced, and absorbing examination of some of the most significant events in U.S. history.

Other notable features contained within each volume in the series include a glossary of important individuals, places, and terms; a detailed chronology featuring page references to relevant sections of the narrative; an annotated bibliography of sources for further study; an extensive general bibliography that reflects the wide range of historical sources consulted by the author; and a subject index.

Acknowledgements

This series was developed in consultation with a distinguished Advisory Board comprised of public librarians, school librarians, and educators. They evaluated the series as it developed, and their comments and suggestions were invaluable throughout the production process. Any errors in this and other volumes in the series are ours alone. Following is a list of board members who contributed to the *Defining Moments* series:

Gail Beaver, M.A., M.A.L.S.
Adjunct Lecturer, University of Michigan
Ann Arbor, MI

Melissa C. Bergin, L.M.S., NBCT
Niskayuna High School
Niskayuna, NY

Rose Davenport, M.S.L.S., Ed.Specialist
Library Media Specialist
Pershing High School Library
Detroit, MI

Karen Imarisio, A.M.L.S.
Assistant Head of Adult Services
Bloomfield Twp. Public Library
Bloomfield Hills, MI

Nancy Larsen, M.L.S., M.S. Ed.
Library Media Specialist
Clarkston High School
Clarkston, MI

Marilyn Mast, M.I.L.S.
Kingswood Campus Librarian
Cranbrook Kingswood Upper School
Bloomfield Hills, MI

Rosemary Orlando, M.L.I.S.
Assistant Director
St. Clair Shores Public Library
St. Clair Shores, MI

Comments and Suggestions

We welcome your comments on *Defining Moments: Prohibition* and suggestions for other events in U.S. history that warrant treatment in the *Defining Moments* series. Correspondence should be addressed to:

Editor, *Defining Moments*
Omnigraphics, Inc.
615 Griswold
Detroit, MI 48226
E-mail: editorial@omnigraphics.com

HOW TO USE THIS BOOK

Defining Moments: Prohibition provides users with a detailed and authoritative overview of the era, as well as the principal figures involved in this pivotal event in U.S. history. The preparation and arrangement of this volume—and all other books in the *Defining Moments* series—reflect an emphasis on providing a thorough and objective account of events that shaped our nation, presented in an easy-to-use reference work.

Defining Moments: Prohibition is divided into three primary sections. The first of these sections, the **Narrative Overview**, provides a detailed, factual account of the Prohibition era. It explores the origins of the Prohibition movement, the political machinations that produced the Eighteenth Amendment, the difficulties of enforcing Prohibition laws, the mob wars that erupted over the alcohol trade, and the social and political forces that finally brought the Prohibition era to a close.

The second section, **Biographies**, provides valuable biographical background on leading figures involved in the era, including crime boss Al Capone, Prohibition leader Wayne B. Wheeler, hatchet-wielding activist Carry Nation, and President Warren G. Harding. Each biography concludes with a list of sources for further information on the profiled individual.

The third section, **Primary Sources**, collects essential and enlightening documents from the Prohibition era, including reminiscences of leading smugglers and speakeasy owners, *Chicago Tribune* coverage of the Valentine's Day Massacre, and the full text of the Eighteenth and Twenty-first Amendments. Other primary sources featured in *Defining Moments: Prohibition* include excerpts from official documents, papers, essays, memoirs, and other important works.

Other valuable features in *Defining Moments: Prohibition* include the following:

- Attribution and referencing of primary sources and other quoted material to help guide users to other valuable historical research resources.

- Glossary of Important People, Places, and Terms.

- Detailed Chronology of events with a *see reference* feature. Under this arrangement, events listed in the chronology include a reference to page numbers within the Narrative Overview wherein users can find additional information on the event in question.

- Photographs of the leading figures and major events of the Prohibition era.

- Sources for Further Study, an annotated list of noteworthy Prohibition-related works.

- Extensive bibliography of works consulted in the creation of this book, including books, periodicals, Internet sites, and videotape materials.

- A Subject Index.

IMPORTANT PEOPLE, PLACES, AND TERMS

Lincoln C. Andrews
Assistant Secretary of Treasury in Charge of Prohibition

Anti-Saloon League
Political-action group supporting Prohibition

Association against the Prohibition Amendment
Political-action group opposing Prohibition

Baker, Rev. Purley A.
General Superintendent of the Anti-Saloon League

Borah, William Edgar
United States senator from Idaho who supported Prohibition

Busch, Adolphus
Co-founder of Anheuser-Busch Brewery and opponent of Prohibition

Cannon, Bishop James, Jr.
Member of the executive committee of the Anti-Saloon League

Capone, Al
Organized-crime boss based in Chicago

Colosimo, "Big Jim"
Organized-crime boss based in Chicago

Collins, Sam
Prohibition Director of Kentucky

Coolidge, Calvin
President of the United States, 1923-1929

Daugherty, Harry M.
Attorney General of the United States, 1921-1924

Dever, William
Mayor of Chicago, 1923-27

dramshop
A term for a barroom, used in the 1600s and 1700s

dry
A supporter of Prohibition laws

Edwards, Edward I.
United States senator from New Jersey who opposed Prohibition

Edwards, Rev. Justin
Leader of the American Temperance Society, 1836-1846

Eighteenth Amendment
The amendment to the United States Constitution that prohibited the manufacture, sale, or transportation of intoxicating liquors.

Einstein, Isidor "Izzy"
Agent with the United States Prohibition Unit

Ford, Henry
Chairman of the Ford Motor Company and supporter of Prohibition

Harding, Warren G.
President of the United States, 1921-1923

Haynes, Roy A.
Prohibition Commissioner, 1921-1927

Hobson, Richmond Pearson
United States congressman from Alabama and co-sponsor of the Eighteenth Amendment

Hoover, Herbert
President of the United States, 1929-1933

Genovese, Vito
Organized-crime boss based in New York City

La Guardia, Fiorello
United States congressman from New York who opposed Prohibition; later served as mayor of New York City

Lansky, Meyer
Organized-crime figure based in New York City

Lewis, Dioclesian
Temperance activist who inspired the Women's War of the 1870s

local-option law
A legal statute that restricted or prohibited alcohol within a specific town or county

Luciano, Charles "Lucky"
Organized-crime boss based in New York City

Maranzano, Salvatore
Organized-crime boss based in New York City

Masseria, Giuseppe "Joe the Boss"
Organized-crime boss based in New York City

Mather, Increase
Puritan religious leader during the late 1600s and early 1700s

McConnell, William
Prohibition Director of Pennsylvania

McCoy, Bill
Smuggler credited with starting "Rum Row"

Moran, George "Bugs"
Leader of Chicago's North Side Gang

Nation, Carry
Saloon-smashing Prohbition activist

National Commission on Law Observance and Enforcement
Group appointed by President Hoover in 1929 to investigate Prohibition; also known as the Wickersham Commission

National Prohibition Enforcement Act
The group of laws passed by Congress in support of the Eighteenth Amendment; also known as the Volstead Act

O'Banion, Dion
Leader of Chicago's North Side Gang

progressive movement
A trend at the turn of the twentieth century that saw activists addressing a range of social problems, including poverty, workplace exploitation, alcohol abuse, and political corruption

Prohibition Party
Political group formed in 1869 that called for a constitutional amendment outlawing alcohol

Remus, George
Bootlegger

Roosevelt, Franklin D.
President of the United States, 1933-1945

Rush, Dr. Benjamin
American medical authority who denounced effects of alcohol in 1785

Russell, Rev. Howard Hyde
Founder of the Anti-Saloon League

Sabin, Pauline
Leader of the Women's Organization for National Prohibition Reform

Second Great Awakening
Religious revival that swept the United States in the 1830s and 1840s

Siegel, Ben "Bugsy"
Organized-crime figure based in New York City

Smith, Al
Governor of New York and Democratic presidential candidate

Smith, Moe
Agent with the United States Prohibition Unit

Sunday, Rev. Billy
Evangelist and anti-alcohol crusader

Talley, Alfred J.
Judge of the United States Court of Sessions who testified before Congress about the negative effects of Prohibition

Thompson, William "Big Bill"
Mayor of Chicago, 1915-23 and 1927-1931

Thompson, Eliza J. "Mother"
Leader of the Women's War of the 1870s

Torrio, Johnny
Organized-crime boss based in Chicago

Twenty-first Amendment
The amendment to the United States Constitution that repealed the Eighteenth Amendment and ended Prohibition

Volstead, Andrew
United States congressman from Minnesota who sponsored the National Prohibition Enforcement Act (the Volstead Act)

Volstead Act
See National Prohibition Enforcement Act

Webb-Kenyon Law
Legislation passed in 1913 that outlawed the shipment of alcohol into dry states.

Weiss, Hymie
Leader of Chicago's North Side Gang

wet
An opponent of Prohibition-era restrictions on alcohol

Wheeler, Wayne B.
General Counsel and National Legislative Superintendent of the Anti-Saloon League

Wickersham, George W.
Chairman of the National Commission on Law Observance and Enforcement

Wickersham Commission
See National Commission on Law Observance and Enforcement

Willard, Frances Elizabeth
President of the National Women's Christian Temperance Union (WCTU)

Willebrandt, Mabel Walker
Assistant Attorney General of the United States, 1921-1929

Wilson, Woodrow
President of the United States, 1913-1921

Women's Organization for National Prohibition Reform
Political-action group opposing Prohibition

Women's War
Anti-alcohol crusade led by female activists in the 1870s

CHRONOLOGY

1893

May 24, 1893 – Rev. Howard Hyde Russell launches the Anti-Saloon League of Ohio. *See p. 19.*

1895

December 17-18, 1895 – The Anti-Saloon League of America is formed at a meeting in Washington, D.C. *See p. 19.*

1907

Georgia and Oklahoma become the first states in the twentieth century to prohibit alcohol. *See p. 22.*

1908

Mississippi and North Carolina enact Prohibition laws.

1909

Tennessee outlaws alcohol.

1912

West Virginia adds an amendment prohibiting alcohol to the state constitution.

1913

February 28-March 1, 1913 – The House and Senate override a presidential veto to pass the Webb-Kenyon Law prohibiting shipment of alcohol into dry states. *See p. 25.*

November 13, 1913 – The Anti-Saloon League adopts a resolution calling for a constitutional amendment prohibiting the manufacture, sale, importation, exportation, and transportation of alcoholic beverages. *See p. 24.*

December 10, 1913 – A resolution for a constitutional amendment prohibiting alcohol is introduced in both houses of the United States Congress. *See p. 26.*

1914

Arizona, Colorado, Oregon, Virginia, and Washington enact statewide Prohibition laws.

August 2, 1914 – The German army invades Luxembourg, effectively beginning World War I. *See p. 26.*

November 3, 1914 – Additional supporters of the dry cause are elected to the House and Senate. *See p. 26.*

December 22, 1914 – The Prohibition amendment resolution comes before a vote in the House of Representatives. There are 197 votes in favor of passage, 190 against, but the resolution fails to reach the necessary two-thirds majority for passage. *See p. 26.*

1915

Alabama, Arkansas, Idaho, Iowa, and South Carolina prohibit alcohol.

1916

Michigan, Montana, Nebraska, and South Dakota enact Prohibition laws.

November 7, 1916 – Anti-alcohol candidates win additional congressional seats. Democrat Woodrow Wilson is reelected to a second term as president. *See p. 26.*

1917

Indiana, New Hampshire, New Mexico, and Utah join the ranks of "dry" states.

April 6, 1917 – The United States declares war on Germany. *See p. 27.*

August 1, 1917 – A revised amendment resolution prohibiting alcohol is passed by a two-thirds majority in the Senate, 65 votes in favor, 20 against. *See p. 30.*

September 8, 1917 – The wartime Food Control Bill takes effect, prohibiting the manufacture of distilled liquor. *See p. 29.*

December 18, 1917 – An amendment resolution prohibiting alcohol is passed by the House of Representatives by a 282-128 vote. The Prohibition amendment is referred to the states for ratification. *See p. 30.*

1918

Florida, Nevada, Ohio, Texas, and Wyoming adopt statewide Prohibition.

January 8, 1918 – Mississippi becomes the first state to ratify the Prohibition amendment to the United States Constitution. *See p. 30.*

November 11, 1918 – The Armistice goes into effect, ending World War I.

1919

Kentucky outlaws alcohol.

January 14, 1919 – Nebraska becomes the thirty-sixth state to ratify the Prohibition amendment. Two days later it officially becomes the Eighteenth Amendment to the United States Constitution. *See p. 30.*

October 28, 1919 – The National Prohibition Enforcement Act (the Volstead Act) becomes law when the Senate joins the House in overriding President Wilson's veto. *See p. 55.*

1920

January 17, 1920 – National Prohibition takes effect. *See p. 31.*

January 31, 1920 – The director of the Customs Service notifies Congress that large amounts of alcohol are being smuggled across U.S. borders and requests additional funds to combat the problem.

November 2, 1920 – Republican Warren G. Harding is elected president of the United States.

December 29, 1920 – Attorney General A. Mitchell Palmer tells the House Appropriations Committee that "it is totally and absolutely impossible" to successfully prosecute Prohibition cases without additional funds and personnel.

1921

August 15, 1921 – Federal and state officials begin the first organized "drive" against smugglers. It has limited success. Others initiatives follow at the rate of about one per year until 1925.

1922

December 8, 1922 – In his message to Congress, President Harding assesses Prohibition and declares that "there are conditions relating to its enforcement which savor of nation-wide scandal."

1923

August 23, 1923 – President Harding dies of a heart attack; Calvin Coolidge becomes president.

1924

March 28, 1924 – Attorney General Harry M. Daugherty resigns his post at the request of President Coolidge. *See p. 60.*

November 4, 1924 – Calvin Coolidge is elected to another term as president.

1925

March 1925 – Johnny Torrio turns his Chicago operation over to Al Capone. *See p. 72.*

April 1, 1925 – General Lincoln C. Andrews is appointed assistant secretary of treasury in charge of Prohibition. *See p. 80.*

1927

April 1, 1927 – The Prohibition Unit is reorganized as the Prohibition Bureau, and Civil Service hiring guidelines are applied to its employees. *See p. 80.*

May 1927 – Dr. James M. Doran becomes Prohibition commissioner, replacing Roy Haynes. Seymour Lowman replaces Lincoln C. Andrews as assistant secretary of treasury in charge of Prohibition.

September 5, 1927 – Wayne Wheeler of the Anti-Saloon League dies of a heart attack. *See p. 82.*

1928

November 6, 1928 – Republican Herbert Hoover is elected president over Democratic candidate Al Smith. *See p. 84*

1929

February 14, 1929 – The Valentine's Day Massacre takes place in Chicago. *See p. 3, 74.*

May 1929 – The Women's Organization for National Prohibition Reform is founded. *See p. 82.*

May 16, 1929 — Al Capone is arrested in Philadelphia for unlawful possession of a firearm. The next day he is sentenced to one year in prison on the weapons charge. *See p. 74.*

May 20, 1929 – President Hoover forms the National Commission on Law Observance and Enforcement (the Wickersham Commission) to investigate issues surrounding Prohibition. *See p. 86.*

October 29, 1929 – The "Black Tuesday" stock-market crash takes place, the first of several economic developments that result in the Great Depression. *See p. 89.*

1931

January 7, 1931 – The National Commission on Law Observance and Enforcement issues its final report. *See p. 86.*

April and September, 1931 – A series of gangland assassinations makes "Lucky" Luciano a central figure in American organized crime. *See p. 77.*

October 24, 1931 – Al Capone is convicted of income tax evasion and sentenced to eleven years in prison. *See p. 75.*

1932

November 8, 1932 – Democrat Franklin D. Roosevelt is elected president, defeating incumbent Herbert Hoover. Democrats gain large majorities in both the House and Senate. *See p. 93.*

December 6, 1932 – A resolution for a constitutional amendment repealing Prohibition is introduced in both houses of Congress. *See p. 93.*

1933

February 16, 1933 – The repeal amendment is passed by a two-thirds majority in the Senate, with 63 votes in favor, 23 against. *See p. 93.*

February 20, 1933 – The amendment is passed by a two-thirds majority in the House, with 289 votes in favor, 121 against. The amendment is referred to the states for ratification. *See p. 93.*

March 13, 1933 – President Roosevelt asks Congress to modify the Volstead Act to allow the sale of 3.2 percent beer. Congress complies with the president's request nine days later. *See p. 93.*

April 7, 1933 – Beer containing 3.2 percent alcohol becomes legal. *See p. 93.*

April 10, 1933 – Michigan becomes the first state to ratify the Twenty-First Amendment. *See p. 93.*

December 5, 1933 – Utah becomes the thirty-sixth state to ratify the proposed amendment repealing Prohibition. The Twenty-First Amendment officially becomes part of the United States Constitution. It repeals the Eighteenth Amendment and ends Prohibition. *See p. 93.*

NARRATIVE OVERVIEW

PROLOGUE

Seven men stood around the percolator inside the dimly lit garage, waiting for their morning coffee. The men wore their hats and coats because it was February in Chicago, and the garage did not have a heater. Even Highball, the dog, looked cold, curled in a ball on the concrete floor.

As they watched the percolator bubble, the men thought about the work ahead. A truck shipment of illegal whiskey was scheduled to arrive later that morning, and their boss, George "Bugs" Moran, had told them to be at the garage to help unload it. Moran was coming down, too, but he was running late. Finally, the backdoor opened, and the assembled men turned to welcome Moran.

Instead, two policemen walked in, guns drawn and shouting orders. The seven men in the garage did what they were told. They lined up facing the wall, hands up. One of the officers went down the line and confiscated all of their guns. Then the seven just stood there facing the wall, their breath puffing out into the cold air, waiting for the cops to arrest them or shake them down. There were more footsteps, and Highball started growling. Then the captured men heard the soft but terrible click of a machine gun being prepared for use.

Authorities later found six of them lying together, shot to pieces. The seventh had managed to crawl twenty feet and was still breathing, but he expired a short time later. Seven dead in a few short machine-gun bursts and two shotgun blasts. It was big news, even in a town that had seen more than 200 gang-related murders in the previous three years. The date had something to do with the memorable nature of the event, too—February 14, 1929. The "Valentine's Day Massacre," as the slaughter came to be called, was a colorful term that people did not forget.

At first, statements from neighbors about the presence of police in the vicinity of the garage led investigators to believe that police officers carried out the slayings. A federal official, Frederick D. Silloway, announced that "the murderers were not gangsters. They were Chicago policemen." But Silloway was wrong. Investigators eventually learned that the massacre was rooted in the long-running feud between Moran and fellow mobster Al Capone.

The rival gang leaders had been at war with one another for years. For the most part, the war consisted of random assassinations, but by 1929 Capone had grown weary of such low-intensity warfare. He turned the vexing Moran "problem" over to "Machine Gun" Jack McGurn, one of his soldiers. It was McGurn who subsequently devised the plan that triggered the massacre. First, he arranged for someone to contact Bugs Moran with a false story that a truckload of Old Log Cabin whiskey had been hijacked and was available for purchase. Moran agreed to the buy and told the man to deliver the truck to a garage at 2122 North Clark Street at 10:30 a.m. in downtown Chicago. McGurn placed three lookouts in rented rooms overlooking the Clark Street garage. Their job was to make sure that Moran and all of his men arrived at the garage before contacting the assassins, who were disguised as policemen.

Although the scheme failed to slay the tardy Moran, it worked smoothly in other respects. The police disguises fooled Moran's men into thinking that a raid was taking place, so they put up little resistance. Once Moran's crew was disarmed by the police lookalikes, three more of McGurn's men entered the garage. Two of them were armed with machine guns.

The Valentine's Day Massacre stunned the American public. It also prompted a somber reassessment of events that had taken place across the country over the previous decade. Ten years earlier, in January 1919, a new amendment had been added to the United States Constitution. The Eighteenth Amendment, which outlawed the manufacture, sale, and transportation of alcoholic beverages, launched the period in American history known as Prohibition (1920-1933).

That single amendment created a profound change in American life in the years following its passage. Millions of citizens became regular lawbreakers. Thousands of law-enforcement officers became corrupted by payoffs. Hundreds of bootleggers became enormously wealthy by providing illegal booze, and gang-related violence over the profits of illegal alcohol escalated. The events of the 1920s and 1930s showed that a constitutional amendment could have many unintended effects. It could, in fact, turn the nation's streets into a battleground.

4

Chapter One

EVENTS LEADING UP TO PROHIBITION

◄━━◖◗━━►

"My Christian Brother, be kind and benevolent like God, and do not spoil his good work. He made wine to gladden the heart of men."—Benjamin Franklin

"[King Alcohol] has occasioned more than three-fourths of the pauperism, three-fourths of the crime, and more than half of the insanity in the community, and thereby filled our prisons, our alms-houses and lunatic asylums.... He has destroyed the lives of tens of thousands of our citizens annually in the most merciless manner."

—*National Temperance Almanac*, 1876

Looking back on the thirteen years of Prohibition—1920 to 1933— many view it as a distant relic of the past. In truth, the roots of Prohibition are even more distant. The string of events that culminated in the passage of the Eighteenth Amendment actually began as soon as the British colonies were established in North America.

Alcohol in Colonial America

Judged by its early history, the United States was an unlikely place to outlaw alcohol. The early colonists from England brought with them a well-developed taste for intoxicating beverages, and drinking became an important part of life in the New World. Alcohol was consumed while relaxing and socializing, but it was also drunk at times and in places that would raise a lot of eyebrows today. Businesses and offices in many colonial towns took daily breaks at eleven a.m. and four p.m. so that everyone could retire to the tavern for a bit of cheer. Workday drinking also was commonplace in the fields. According to historian Herbert Asbury in *The Great Illusion*, "it was generally agreed that no man could do a day's work on a farm without alcoholic stimulation." Most farmers provided liquor for their hired hands, and those who failed to do so were likely to find themselves short of workers. Slaves were often provided with a ration of strong drink as well. Alcohol was especially prevalent at community gatherings, such as those to cut wood and raise barns.

The widespread acceptance of drinking did not mean that communities were blind to the problem of alcohol abuse, however. Many towns maintained laws that dictated the amount of alcohol that could be purchased at one time and placed limitations on public drinking. In the Massachusetts Bay Colony, for instance, it was considered excessive to drink "more than half a pint at one time," and customers who spent "above ye space of half an hour" in the tavern were in violation of the law. But on the whole, drinking was a widely accepted part of daily life. Even the morally strict Puritans who settled in New England did not outlaw alcohol, though they did take a dim view of those who became visibly inebriated.

In fact, a person who *did not* drink was usually viewed with more suspicion than someone who did. Alcohol accompanied most social and business functions, and those who did not imbibe were outsiders. In addition to greasing the wheels of public interaction, liquor was believed to provide a boost of energy, ward off disease, and cure a variety of ailments. It was considered harmless enough that it was commonly given to babies (sometimes mixed with opium).

The prevalence of alcohol partly stemmed from the trade system that made the North American colonies profitable. Rum was the most common spirit during the colonial era, and it played a crucial role in the so-called triangular trade system. In this system, merchants obtained molasses from the sugar plantations in the Caribbean. The molasses was distilled into rum in North America, especially in Rhode Island and Massachusetts, then shipped to Africa to be traded for slaves. The slaves were then taken to the Caribbean and exchanged for molasses, completing the cycle. Not all of the rum produced was sent to Africa, however. Much was kept for consumption in North America, where it was plentiful and cheap. Favorite colonial drinks included the rum flip (a heated mixture of rum, beer, and sugar or molasses), the rum sling (rum, water, and sugar), and rum punch (rum, spices, and lime or lemon juice).

Apple cider that had fermented into an alcoholic drink was the second-most popular choice. Most farm families produced their own "hard" cider, so it tended to be served in homes more often than taverns. Whiskey, which was distilled from grain rather than molasses, made its appearance in the late 1700s and became an important commodity in remote regions such as western Pennsylvania. Farmers in those areas faced difficulties in transporting bushels of grain by horseback on the rough backcountry roads. It proved more profitable to distill a portion of their crop (corn, rye, or barley) into whiskey, which was easier to transport and quite lucrative.

"Wine is from God," said Puritan leader Increase Mather. "But the drunkard is from the devil."

Though precise numbers are hard to come by, it is clear that Americans were consuming a lot of alcohol in the late eighteenth and early nineteenth centuries. In the early decades of the 1800s, several groups urging responsible drinking tried to estimate the average person's consumption based on liquor sales. Though the numbers varied widely between locations, the lowest figure was almost 2.3 gallons of distilled spirits per person per year. In the city with the highest average (Albany, New York) the estimate was ten gallons per person.

The Fight for Temperance

Americans may have been fond of drink, but they were also deeply religious. The two loyalties did not always sit well together. Early in the colonial period, some religious leaders suggested that those who paid too much attention to alcohol were paying too little attention to God. One was Puritan leader Increase Mather, who stated in 1673 that "the flood of excessive drinking will drown Christianity." Mather did not expect people to give up alcohol completely. He simply wanted them to use it more responsibly. "Wine is from God," he said in one sermon, "but the drunkard is from the devil." Temperance (moderate use of alcohol) rather than prohibition (completely outlawing alcohol) remained the focus of reformers up until the 1830s. Most who urged temperance were opposed to distilled liquor such as rum (often called "ardent spirits" at the time) but had little quarrel with lighter forms of alcohol such as cider, beer, and wine.

In 1785 Benjamin Rush published an influential tract condemning alcohol and its impact on public health.

In the 1780s the temperance movement took a big step forward with the help of medical science. Dr. Benjamin Rush was one of the best-known medical authorities in the newly formed United States and had served as the surgeon general of the Continental Army during the American Revolution. In 1785 he published a pamphlet entitled *An Inquiry into the Effect of Spirituous Liquors on the Human Body and Mind*. It debunked the widespread belief that alcohol promoted good health. Instead, Rush argued that liquor had little medicinal or nutritional value and that it caused a range of diseases.

Judged against modern medical knowledge, Rush was wrong on many counts (such as his claim that drinking caused epilepsy). But his book was very influential, and it was the first of several notable science-based attacks on alcohol. Some of these were inaccurate and sensational. Dr. Eliphalet Nott, the president of Union College, was one of many medical authorities who claimed that a heavy drinker was likely to burst into flames, consumed by "internal fires, kindled often spontaneously in the fumes of alcohol." Other criticisms were proven true, however. By the 1860s, it was shown that alcohol did not keep the body warm, as had been widely believed, and in the 1890s, alcohol was found to be a depressant rather than a stimulant.

Benjamin Rush's theories helped jump-start the formal temperance movement. Groups dedicated to promoting the responsible use of alcohol formed as early as 1789. Many of them were short-lived, but in the mid-1820s, an effective national organization called the American Temperance Society was established under the direction of Rev. Justin Edwards. The society evolved into the American Temperance Union in 1836, though the new group should perhaps have come up with a different name for itself. Rather than urging temperance, the union took a new course and began to urge people to abstain completely from alcohol of all types. The idea that alcohol could be completely prohibited began to be discussed more widely in American society around this time.

Laws of God and Man

In addition to being a masterful organizer, Justin Edwards pioneered a new approach in the campaign against alcohol. Edwards, along with Rev. Lyman Beecher and others, made the abolition of liquor into a religious crusade by promoting the idea that drinking was a sin that doomed people to hell. Prior to that point, the temperance reformers had concentrated on the difficulties that alcohol caused on earth, including broken homes, increased poverty, and misspent lives. Under the arguments put forth by Edwards and the others, the bottle caused eternal damage.

This was an important development on the road to Prohibition. After all, the Bible makes a lot of positive references to alcoholic beverages, the best known being Jesus's miracle of transforming water into wine. To claim that drinking that same beverage could send you to the depths of hell was a new interpreta-

An 1851 Currier & Ives print extolling American men and women dedicated to temperance.

tion of scripture. It was well received by many Christians, however, partly because it fit so well with the times. The 1830s and 1840s saw the coming of the Second Great Awakening—a period of increased religious devotion that was marked by large revivalist meetings. The movement reflected a fundamental change in religious ideas and had far-reaching implications. Previously, the Calvinist tradition had maintained that salvation was largely in God's hands. The Second Great Awakening helped further the theory that people could take an active role in achieving salvation by watching their own behavior. Drinking became identified as one of the sins that needed to be stamped out, and revival preachers personally called on drinkers to give up the bottle.

Activists employed another weapon in their battle against ardent spirits—legislation. In the 1840s temperance forces were successful in backing laws that restricted or banned the sale of alcohol in many local communities. In 1851 Maine passed a strict law prohibiting the sale and manufacture of alcoholic beverages throughout the state. By 1855 thirteen other states and territories had passed similar measures. A wave of temperance seemed to be sweeping the nation.

As time passed, however, the temperence movement was eclipsed by the rising tensions over slavery. By the late 1850s, the dispute over the use of slave labor in the southern states was reaching a crisis point and would soon lead to the Civil War. Many of the same reformers who led the battle against alcohol were also dedicated abolitionists. As they became preoccupied with the war and the issues that sparked it, the campaign against alcohol waned and then lost ground. Almost all of the statewide temperance laws were repealed. The Civil War harmed the anti-alcohol movement in another way, as well. In order to raise money for the conflict, the U.S. Congress passed the Internal Revenue Act in 1862. This act, which levied heavy taxes on the sale of alcohol, remained in effect after the war ended. For the next half-century, one of the strongest arguments against Prohibition was that it would eliminate these vital tax dollars.

The temperance issue never went away, but it receded into the background until after the Civil War ended. One of the first signs of its resurgence was the founding of the Prohibition Party in 1869. This group fielded its own political candidates on a platform that called for a constitutional amendment outlawing alcohol. The party's presidential nominees in the 1870s and 1880s were not serious contenders, but they helped make alcohol an election issue. By the 1890s support for the party had faded, but its leaders soldiered on. In fact, the party still exists today, though it has few members.

Women Join the Fight

The next offensive on alcohol was the so-called Women's War of the 1870s. The movement was sparked by reformer Dioclesian Lewis, who promoted the idea of staging protests at places where alcohol was sold. On Christmas Eve 1873, Eliza J. "Mother" Thompson and seventy followers put Lewis's ideas into action in Hillsboro, Ohio. Employing the same non-violent tactics that would later be used in protests over civil rights and the Vietnam War, they marched on a town drugstore that sold alcohol. Confronted by dozens of singing and praying women, the store's owner quickly surrendered. When he issued his promise to stop selling liquor, the crusade was off and running.

The protests spread to other towns in Ohio, then across the Midwest, and even as far as California. Not all battles were as easily won as the first

WOMAN'S HOLY WAR.
Grand Charge on the Enemy's Works.

This 1874 lithograph reflects the leading role women played in the crusade for temperance and prohibition.

Hillsboro engagement. The women were sprayed with water and showered with eggs and beer at some protests. But they registered many triumphs as well. In fact, the Women's War closed an estimated 25,000 drinking establishments across the country before it lost momentum. New saloons quickly replaced those that had closed, but the publicity surrounding the movement helped reenergize the fight against alcohol. It also showed that large numbers of women were willing to oppose alcohol visibly and vocally.

A number of forceful women activists followed in Mother Thompson's footsteps. One was Frances Elizabeth Willard, who became president of a new organization, the national Women's Christian Temperance Union (WCTU), that had been formed in 1874. The group's greatest accomplishment was to convince schools all across the country to begin anti-alcohol education programs. These had an immense impact on school children over the course of several decades. At the direction of the WCTU, many kindergarten students were taught to chant "Tremble King Alcohol, we shall grow up!" It was a threat that proved true: after reaching adulthood many of those children would look favorably upon the passage of Eighteenth Amendment.

The WCTU was also the starting point for the most famous female firebrand of the era—Carry Nation (see biography on Nation, p. 122). Initially, Nation adhered to the group's policy of peaceful opposition to alcohol, but she eventually decided to take things a step further. Armed with a hatchet, she took to marching into saloons unannounced and smashing them to bits. In the first years of the 1900s, she spread a swath of destruction from her home state of Kansas to New York City. Nation attributed her saloon assaults to the fact that her first husband was an alcoholic, and tales of this type gave a lot of authority to the women who fought against alcohol. One of the most persuasive arguments in favor of Prohibition was that alcohol disrupted family life. When men spent precious money on beer or failed to hold a job because of their drinking, it was their wives who suffered the most.

Taverns, Saloons, and Politics

The chief targets of Mother Thompson, Carry Nation, and other reformers were the nation's barrooms, where men—and men only—drank their beer and liquor. The development of public drinking houses in America played a large role in the Prohibition saga. They became a fixture in North America soon after the arrival of European settlers in the 1620s. Initially, such places

Members of the Women's Christian Temperance Union march in Washington, D.C. in support of Prohibition.

were known as taverns or dramshops (a "dram" being a measure of drink); later they became known as saloons—a term used all across the United States, not just in western towns. During the first century of the colonial era, most taverns provided a community-oriented atmosphere. Town meetings and court trials were held there, and proprietors were generally well-respected figures. Most provided food and accommodations in addition to alcohol. All of these qualities tended to make them hubs of community activity as well as drinking establishments.

In the 1700s the nature of the tavern began to change as rum became plentiful and cheap. The number of drinking establishments multiplied, less respected operators came on the scene, and competition became more intense. In most locations, a tavern owner needed a license to sell alcohol legally. Deciding how many licenses were to be issued and who would get them was the business of government. Not surprisingly, this arrangement spawned numerous unsavory relationships between local politicians and alcohol distributors. In time, taverns and saloons became synonymous with political corruption.

In their simplest form, the shady practices occurred because the saloon or tavern owner needed assistance from politicians to stay in business, and the politicians needed votes to stay in office. Barkeepers became proficient at delivering votes for candidates that gave them a hand, and the votes usually came from the saloon's customers. In some cases, men might be induced to vote for a certain candidate simply because the saloonkeeper was a persuasive opinion maker, but blatant vote buying became common, with men trading their votes for alcohol, money, or other favors. In some cities, saloon owners were so influential that they became political bosses in their own right, exerting a great deal of control over city officials and policies.

Opposition to saloon-based corruption hit its peak in the late 1800s and early 1900s, but the problem had started long before. In 1760 John Adams, who would later become president of the United States, complained in his diary about politicians who "multiply taverns and dramshops and thereby secure the votes of taverner and retailer and all; and the multiplication of taverns will make many, who may be induced to flip and rum, to vote for any man whatever."

The Business of Alcohol

By the late 1800s some saloons and taverns had become closely associated with prostitution and gambling. They also came to be increasingly regarded as havens for criminals. This evolving perception was partly attributable to the way the trade was organized. Beginning in the mid-1800s, beer became the most popular drink in the country, and beer brewers became the most powerful figures in the alcohol industry. Unlike today, the breweries of the nineteenth century were actively involved in the retail end of the trade. In some cases they directly owned saloons. In others, an individual might "own" the drinking establishment, but a brewery held the mortgage on the property, paid for the license, and—most importantly—provided the beer. The primary aim of the brewers was to create outlets for their products, so they encouraged the opening of new drinking houses. This led to an overabundance of saloons, which made it hard for the operators to turn a profit.

When their revenue dwindled, some saloon owners turned to illegal activities that would bring in much-needed revenue. Some allowed prostitutes to ply their trade in the bar, while others would solicit business for nearby bordellos. Barkeepers allowed illegal gambling on the premises in return for a cut of the winnings. Many saloons were forced to stay open for extended periods in order to bring in more money, so they ignored local laws that dictated the hours and days they could operate. These illegal activities played into the issue of political corruption: saloons were able to flout the laws because they paid off corrupt politicians and policemen to avoid arrest.

Not every saloon engaged in these practices. In *Prohibition: Thirteen Years That Changed America*, Edward Behr

This wood engraving, titled "The Bar of Destruction," portrays the saloon as a hellish place that lures men away from their rightful place with their families.

notes that reputable places did not tolerate prostitutes and other illegal activity, and that many saloons were more likely to host "perfectly innocent social gatherings involving singing, dancing, and recitations." The better establishments oftentimes also served as a type of social club and as an informal employment agency for men seeking work. Still, the negative connotations of the barroom became so great and pervasive that they came to be seen as an urgent public issue by the close of the nineteenth century. During this time, large numbers of people unaffiliated with the religious crusade against alcohol expressed support for some type of saloon reform.

A Changing Country

The late nineteenth century was a turbulent period in the United States, and many of the changes taking place in other aspects of American life played a role in the debate over alcohol. By the 1870s, industrialism was beginning to transform the way that many Americans worked and lived. Previously, the United States had been a land of farms and small towns. As industries were established, large numbers of people moved to the cities to take jobs in the factories, and they were joined by millions of immigrants. By 1900 two of every five Americans lived in the large cities. Twenty years later, these cities held the majority of the population.

Those who remained in the countryside and small towns viewed this process with apprehension. Residents of small-town America perceived major differences in values between city and country, and they began to fear that they would be overwhelmed by the evils they saw in the large towns. These included crime, prostitution, political corruption, and loose morals. All were associated with alcohol and the saloon in the minds of rural people, so it is little wonder that the countryside became the bedrock of Prohibition. Many people in these areas believed that outlawing alcohol would combat the evils of modernization and help promote wholesome rural traditions.

The immigrants that were swelling the cities became another factor in the debate. Their presence was opposed by many longer-established Americans, who greeted the newcomers with fear and bigotry. Most of the immigrants hailed from parts of Europe where alcohol played a large role in everyday life, and they brought these practices with them. As a result, many people who were opposed to immigration looked favorably on the idea of Prohibition. They saw it as a weapon that might slow the waves of immigration and counter the influence of the newcomers. Adding fuel to this fire was the issue of religion. Many of the immigrants were Catholics. The majority of those active in the temperance movement were Protestants. The conflict between the two religious groups had fueled the wars of Europe for

America's First Attempt to Prohibit Alcohol

Shortly after the colony of Georgia was established in 1733, its leader, General James Oglethorpe, notified the colonists that they should drink nothing stronger than beer. The general was worried that the use of ardent spirits would make the colonists less productive. Oglethorpe's pronouncement was ignored, and Georgia was soon awash with rum and brandy, some of it distilled by the colonists, some of it imported from South Carolina and other British holdings in the New World. The colony's trustees in England became concerned by the "excessive drinking of rum punch" in Georgia and sought assistance from Parliament. In 1735, an act took effect that outlawed the "importation of rums and brandies" into Georgia (beer was still allowed). The first battle between a Prohibition law and thirsty Americans was joined.

The law lost. Moonshine stills were soon brewing up hooch in the Georgia backwoods. Rumrunners brought in boatloads of liquor from colonies farther north. Homes and stores became illegal drinking houses. When the government tried to crack down on the lawbreakers, they met with opposition from the colonists. Most juries refused to convict those accused of violating the act. In addition, some government officials accepted payoffs to ignore the bootleg trade in alcohol.

British authorities eventually saw that the act was a failure, and it was abandoned in 1742. During the seven years it had been in effect, liquor had continued to flow into Georgia in large amounts. The lure of bootlegging profits had drawn many people away from the other business of the colony, contributed to official corruption, and led to a general disregard for the law. These same problems would appear on a much larger scale during the Prohibition era of the 1920s and early 1930s.

centuries, and there was plenty of hostility between the groups in North America as well.

Small-town residents were not the only ones worried about the changes in America. The so-called progressive movement drew together reformers who sought to fix a range of significant problems afflicting the American citizenry, including political corruption, unsafe work conditions, and the seemingly limitless power of large corporations. Progressive activists were especially concerned about the overcrowded and badly polluted slums in America's big cities. In seeking ways to improve the lives of the people who lived in these areas—many of them newly arrived immigrants—reformers often focused on alcohol and the destructive impact of alcohol abuse on families. Some believed that eliminating liquor would greatly improve the lives of the urban poor.

As the 1800s drew to a close, the stage was set for the battle over Prohibition. On one side of the issue were the so-called "drys," who opposed alcohol or at least sought some type of reform. (The term "dry" stemmed from their crusade to "dry up" the flood of alcohol.) The drys included dedicated religious activists who viewed alcohol reform as the most important social and moral issue of the time as well as less zealous people who had become alarmed by the negative aspects of the saloon. On the other side of the issue were the "wets," who believed no new legal limitations should be placed on alcohol. In this camp were those that had a clear financial stake in the drink trade: brewers, distillers, and saloon owners. They were joined by people who believed that consuming alcohol was a basic American right, as well as those who believed that laws prohibiting alcohol would prove unworkable. Up until the late 1800s, the dry cause had gained little ground because they had been unable to overcome the political clout of the wets. That was about to change.

Chapter Two

OUTLAWING ALCOHOL

—⟨⟨⟨⟨ ♪ ⟩⟩⟩⟩—

"Whenever I passed a saloon I sent up a prayer, 'O, God, stop this!' At length God plainly said to me, 'You know how to do it; go and help answer your own prayers.'"

—Rev. Howard Hyde Russell, founder
of the Anti-Saloon League

In 1893, in the town of Oberlin, Ohio, a new temperance organization was formed. The Anti-Saloon League of Ohio was the idea of Rev. Howard Hyde Russell, a graduate of Oberlin College and a veteran activist in the fight against alcohol. Russell's plan was to form a group that would remain independent of the existing political parties and would not become a political party in its own right, as was the case with the Prohibition Party. Instead, it would offer its support to any political candidate that would agree to oppose alcohol, and its focus would be strictly limited to the issue of temperance. Activists in other states latched onto Russell's idea, forming their own chapters. In 1895 the various state groups joined together to establish the Anti-Saloon League of America, with Russell as its first acting director. This was the group that would eventually turn the political tide in favor of Prohibition.

The Anti-Saloon League (ASL) was dedicated to stamping out all forms of alcohol, and it would eventually lobby for national Prohibition. But in choosing its name, the group's leaders showed the shrewd political judgement that they would display repeatedly in the years to come. They knew they could attract more people to their cause if they first championed a cause that enjoyed wide public support—opposing the saloon and its perceived negative impact on communities—rather than the more radical goal of making alcohol illegal.

From the beginning, the ASL had a strong association with religious groups. It even adopted the slogan "the church in action against the saloon." Many of its staff members were drawn from the clergy, and local churches were used to communicate its message and raise money. Though it was open to religions of all types, core support came from Protestants, with the Methodist churches being the strongest group, followed by Baptists and Presbyterians. Members of these churches had been promoting temperance for decades, but the ASL was able to organize their efforts and direct them more forcefully toward a political solution to the alcohol problem.

Playing Politics

That process took time. It was not until the first decade of the 1900s that the ASL really began to make its presence felt in the political arena. By that time, Russell had stepped down, and Rev. Purley A. Baker became the group's general superintendent. It was another ASL official who proved the most powerful figure in the fight for Prohibition, however. Wayne B. Wheeler had joined the Ohio chapter of the group in 1894 (see biography on Wheeler, p. 138). He then became an early and skilled practitioner of the sort of hard-nosed political tactics that the league would later employ nationwide.

The ASL strategy utilized by Wheeler and his cohorts developed as follows: In elections for local, state, and national office, the ASL asked Democratic and Republican candidates for their views on alcohol. If both supported the dry cause, the ASL would take no further action in the race. If one was dry and the other wet, the ASL put its full support behind the anti-alcohol candidate. In cases where both major-party candidates were wet, the league would sponsor an independent candidate who supported temperance. The ASL considered the politician's stance on alcohol to be the only relevant issue. Other policies were ignored, and personal conduct was unimportant. It was not unusual for the ASL to back a known drinker so long as the candidate proclaimed himself in favor of the dry positions. In one Ohio election, the ASL even endorsed a saloon owner who promised to vote in line with their desires.

The support the league gave to the candidates they chose could be considerable. ASL members would blanket a district to assist in the campaign, distributing vast amounts of literature promoting the candidate and the dry cause in general. The ASL placed great stock in the written word—the mass media of the day. The organization established its own publishing company to churn out pamphlets and periodicals in huge numbers. In addition to millions of pages of election-related flyers, the ASL published a daily newspaper, two weekly papers, two monthly papers, and a quarterly journal—all of them distributed nationwide. The ASL also specialized in spreading negative information about opposing candidates, some of which was exaggerated or simply untrue. Speaking of his political activities, William E. "Pussyfoot" Johnson, a famed ASL operative, confessed that "I have told enough lies for the cause to make Ananias [a notorious liar in the New Testament] ashamed of himself. The lies that I have told would fill a big book."

Wayne Wheeler emerged as an influential power-broker for the Anti-Saloon League in the early twentieth century.

When lobbying and mudslinging failed, money sometimes succeeded. According to Wheeler, the ASL spent $35 million between 1893 and 1926 to promote their cause, a huge sum in that era. The league's funds came from both the wealthy and the humble. Small-change contributions solicited in church visits totaled as much as $2 million annually. These contributions were enhanced by large gifts from wealthy industrialists such as Henry Ford, Pierre Du Pont, John D. Rockefeller Sr., and his son, John Jr. The Rockefellers alone contributed $350,000 to the league between 1900 and 1926. While some of these men were inspired by religious ideals, they shared the belief that industrial productivity—and hence their personal fortunes—would increase if alcohol became less available to workers.

While some of these funds were used for legitimate purposes, most historians believe that the ASL used its money illegally at times—most commonly by "buying" politicians so they would support the league's policies. Such activities were not unusual in turn-of-the-twentieth-century American politics. While it is difficult to judge how widespread these practices were, the ASL seemed to manage the process skillfully: No proof of corrupt practices was ever brought forth against them. In many cases, however, payoffs of this kind were unnecessary. The ASL had built its supporters into a powerful voting bloc that struck fear in the hearts of many politicians at election time.

Drying up the States

The ASL's activities showed impressive results. After electing a sizable number of dry candidates in local elections, it focused on passing "local option" laws, which prohibited alcohol within a specific town or county. Large patches of the country went dry in this fashion in the early 1900s. Then the league moved its efforts to the state level. The ASL scored its first major victories in 1907, when Georgia and Oklahoma went dry. It was the beginning of a trend. Over the next twelve years, twenty-eight more states restricted alcohol in some fashion. Some states passed strict or "bone-dry" measures, while others were more lenient—prohibiting the sale of alcohol, for instance, but not its importation or manufacture.

Most states that opted for their own form of Prohibition had something in common: they were largely rural, non-industrial states in the South, the West, and the Midwest. This was further proof of the city/country division over alcohol. Small-town America provided the strongest backing for Prohibition, while the nation's biggest cities were generally opposed to it. Had the drys kept their focus on state and local campaigns, it is doubtful that areas with large urban populations would have ever opted to become dry. Not surprisingly, the big cities would prove very hostile to national Prohibition once it was forced upon them.

American brewers and distillers gradually came to realize that the ASL posed a dangerous threat to their livelihoods. In 1907 an industry publication described the league as "a strongly centralized organization, officered by men with unusual ability, financiered by capitalists with very long purses, subscribed to by hundreds of thousands of men, women, and children who are solicited by their various churches." Alcohol manufacturers did not sit idle while the fight for Prohibition was waged; they simply got beat. The actions they took were ineffective, and in some cases they hurt their cause more than they helped it.

Like the ASL, the brewers and distillers spent a lot of money attempting to control elections. Beer kingpins such as Adolphus Busch (of Anheuser-Busch) targeted money directly at crucial campaigns around the country.

Using Prejudice to Fight Alcohol

Dry forces played upon racial and ethnic fears to further their cause. This was especially true in the South. There was a widespread belief among southern whites that black men were a dangerous threat to white women, and that the danger increased when blacks had been drinking. The drys used this idea to promote their cause. Richmond Pearson Hobson, an Alabama congressman and ASL fundraiser, stated that "liquor will actually make a brute out of a negro, causing him to commit unnatural crimes. The effect is the same on the white man, though the white man being further evolved, it takes longer to reduce him to the same level." On another occasion, Hobson, who co-sponsored the first Prohibition resolution in 1913, stated that "in America we are making the last stand of the great white race, and substantially of the human race. If this destroyer [alcohol] can not be conquered in young America, it can not in any of the old and more degenerate nations."

By "degenerate nations," Hobson meant the countries of Europe. The European immigrants that came to the United States were frequently targeted by the drys—partly because most immigrants opposed Prohibition. Often these attacks played upon fears that the newcomers would pollute the "real" America and lead to foreign domination. Alphonso Alva Hopkins, a prominent dry advocate, complained in *Profit and Loss in Man* that "besodden Europe ... sends here her drink-makers, her drunkard-makers, and her drunkards, or her more temperate but habitual drinkers, with all their un-American and anti-American ideas of morality and government.... Foreign control or conquest could gain little more, though secured by foreign armies and fleets." The ASL's Ernest Cherrington employed similar ideas, dismissing German-Americans as "a lot of swill-fattened, blowsy half-foreigners getting together and between hiccoughs laying down definitions to Americans regarding the motive of our constitution and laws."

Such rhetoric was more common in the late 1800s and early 1900s than it is today, but it seems to have been especially common in the Prohibition debate. The topic of alcohol had a knack for touching on the era's other sensitive issues.

Unlike the ASL, however, the alcohol lobby was clumsy when it came to illegal activity, and on several occasions its underhanded activities were exposed. For example, a group of breweries in Texas pleaded guilty to illegal election practices in 1916. The United States Brewers' Association was indicted for similar shenanigans in Pennsylvania in 1918, with the guilty parties paying heavy fines. The ASL, of course, made sure that these corruption charges were widely publicized.

The brewers' biggest misstep was their failure to reform the saloon trade on their own. The crime and corruption associated with the saloons convinced many people to support the dry cause even though they did not favor an outright ban on alcohol. The brewers certainly had the ability to make changes had they wished to. In the early 1900s they controlled an estimated 75 percent of the country's drinking establishments, either directly or indirectly (by holding mortgages on saloon property, for example). Had the brewers made a concentrated effort to clean up the drinking houses in the first decade of the 1900s, they might have been able to slow or stop the anti-alcohol bandwagon. Charles Merz, one of the first historians to look at Prohibition, makes this point in his book *The Dry Decade*. "They might have attempted to protect their business by putting it in order," Merz wrote of the brewers. "They preferred to argue that there was nothing in their business which needed to be put in order and to spend their time and effort creating an elaborate system of protection which toppled to the ground."

In 1916, the alcohol industry realized its error and tried to change course. The United States Brewer's Association took out newspaper ads claiming that they would help reform the saloons and promote "real temperance, which means sobriety and moderation; not prohibition." The National Retail Liquor Dealers' Association took a more feeble approach, vowing to fight against the use of profanity in the saloons. These efforts proved too little and too late. By that point the ASL's push for national Prohibition was hitting high gear.

Amending the Constitution

"The first shot in the battle for the Eighteenth Amendment," as Wayne Wheeler described it, was actually fired in 1913. That year, at the ASL Jubilee Convention in Columbus, Ohio, a resolution was put forth calling for an amendment to the United States Constitution that would prohibit alcohol throughout the nation. This was a large step for the league, but its success in passing anti-alcohol measures in various states had generated a widespread consensus that it was time to take the fight to the next level. In December of that year, resolutions for the amendment were introduced in both houses of Congress.

One of the primary rationales for pursuing nationwide Prohibition was that localized bans on alcohol were only partially effective. Determined drinkers and suppliers found ways to get past the laws. Until 1913, it was legal to ship alcohol from wet areas to dry areas, so long as it was for personal consumption. A large mail-order alcohol business met this demand. Of course, some of the mail-order alcohol was not used for personal consumption at all. Instead, it was resold by bootleggers or served in illegal drinking establishments.

"During the final stages of the battle, there were approximately 50,000 trained speakers, volunteers, and regulars, directing their fire upon wets in every village, town, city, county, and state."

The mail-order trade was outlawed with the 1913 passage of the Webb-Kenyon Law, which expressly prohibited the shipment of alcohol into dry states. But dry states and communities still experienced great difficulty defending their borders. Areas that outlawed alcohol were often close to places where liquor was still legal. It was a relatively simple matter for people to travel to the wet areas to buy alcohol or for bootleggers to ship it into the dry areas in large amounts. The ASL and its allies argued that if the entire nation went dry, the ban could be effectively enforced. Senator William Edgar Borah, quoted in the *New York Times*, complained that state laws banning alcohol were "broken down and trampled under foot by powers outside the state" and contended that "it would be utterly impossible for the state to protect itself unless the national government ... also declared that policy." This theory ignored the fact that, even with national Prohibition, huge amounts of alcohol could be smuggled into the United States from foreign countries.

Amending the United States Constitution is not a simple process, which is why it has only happened twenty-seven times in the nation's history. A resolution such as the one presented in 1913 first needs to be passed by a two-thirds majority in both houses of Congress (rather than by a simple majority, as is the case with regular laws). It then must be ratified by three-fourths of the states (either passed by a statewide convention or approved by a majority of the states' legislators).

The drys needed a lot of votes in Congress to get past the first of these hurdles, and at the outset they did not have the necessary support. When the constitutional resolution was first brought before the House of Representatives in 1914, it received more yes votes than no votes, but it fell far short of the necessary two-thirds majority needed for passage. After this initial failure, the ASL set the resolution aside and buckled down to the task of electing more Prohibition-friendly politicians to Congress.

The congressional elections of 1914 and 1916 proved to be crucial in the adoption of Prohibition. In his recollections of this period, Wayne Wheeler portrayed the ASL as an army at war. "During the final stages of the battle," he wrote of the 1914 election, "there were approximately 50,000 trained speakers, volunteers, and regulars, directing their fire upon the wets in every village, town, city, county, and state." In the 1916 campaign, he recalled, the league "laid down such a barrage as candidates for Congress had never seen before." The Prohibition offensive was a success: In 1914, drys picked up valuable seats in both the House and the Senate. In 1916, twice as many dry candidates were elected to Congress as wets. This congressional turnover provided the ASL with the votes necessary to put the Prohibition amendment before the states. As 1917 dawned, the ASL was winning the political war, and it was about to get a huge boost from a war of a different kind.

Prohibition Effort Aided by World War I

In August 1914, simmering tensions between the powerful nations of Europe reached the crisis point, and the First World War commenced. On one side were the Allies: Great Britain, France, Russia, and—later—Italy. On the other side were the Central Powers: Germany, Austria-Hungary, and Turkey. (Less powerful countries were involved in the war on both sides.) Eventually, the United States would join the fray, but not until 1917, when it joined the Allies. For the first two and a half years of the war, America remained officially neutral.

U.S. neutrality, however, did not prevent the American public from taking sides over the conflict. Given the historic ties between the United States and Great Britain, many Americans sided with the Allies, especially those who were descended from British ancestors. German-Americans, however, had an understandable attachment to the country their ancestors had come from, so many of them supported the German war effort. These antagonisms would have had little to do with the issue of Prohibition except for one important fact: the majority of America's brewery owners were German-Americans.

In April 1917, the U.S. abandoned its neutrality and declared war on Germany and the rest of the Central Powers. Anti-German sentiment grew strong throughout the country, and Americans with ties to Germany came under suspicion of being disloyal to the United States. The drys capitalized on this situation. They did their best to cast suspicion upon brewery owners, most of whom were longtime supporters of the National German-American Alliance, a group that promoted German culture, criticized the British war effort, and opposed U.S. involvement in the

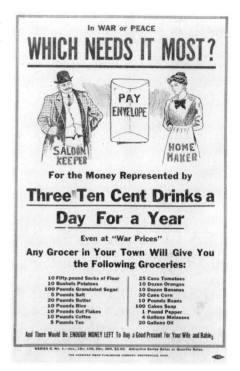

In WAR or PEACE

WHICH NEEDS IT MOST?

PAY ENVELOPE

SALOON KEEPER   HOME MAKER

For the Money Represented by

Three Ten Cent Drinks a
Day For a Year

Even at "War Prices"

**Any Grocer in Your Town Will Give You
the Following Groceries:**

10 Fifty-pound Sacks of Flour	25 Cans Tomatoes
10 Bushels Potatoes	10 Dozen Oranges
100 Pounds Granulated Sugar	10 Dozen Bananas
5 Pounds Salt	30 Cans Corn
20 Pounds Butter	10 Pounds Beans
10 Pounds Rice	100 Cakes Soap
10 Pounds Oat Flakes	1 Pound Pepper
10 Pounds Coffee	4 Gallons Molasses
5 Pounds Tea	20 Gallons Oil

And There Would Be ENOUGH MONEY LEFT To Buy a Good Present For Your Wife and Babies

SERIES G. No. 1.—doz., 10c; 100, 50c; 500, $2.00. Attractive Series Rates or Quantity Rates.
THE AMERICAN ISSUE PUBLISHING COMPANY, WESTERVILLE, OHIO.

This Prohibition poster shows a list of groceries that could be purchased with money used for alcoholic drinks.

war. Wayne Wheeler convinced members of Congress to launch an investigation of the alliance, and the negative publicity that resulted forced the group to disband. Wheeler also urged the federal government to investigate brewers directly. "It is reported to me that the Anheuser-Busch Company and some of the Milwaukee companies are largely controlled by alien Germans," he reported to A. Mitchell Palmer, who served as the Custodian of Alien Property during the war. These sorts of accusations led to further public ridicule for the brewers, though they were never implicated in treasonous activity.

The ASL's intention was to link alcohol with anti-Americanism and frame Prohibition as a patriotic cause. In one of his many statements on the subject, Wheeler proclaimed that "the liquor traffic aids those forces in our country whose loyalty is called into question at this hour." In another instance, he raised the specter of German leader Kaiser Wilhelm II: "Kaiserism abroad and

What Did Prohibition Prohibit?

To say that alcohol was simply forbidden after passage of the Eighteenth Amendment is misleading. The amendment, combined with the legal statutes in the National Prohibition Enforcement Act (better known as the Volstead Act), outlawed certain actions related to alcohol, but did not outlaw alcohol entirely.

The general provisions of the amendment declared that it was illegal to manufacture, sell, transport, import, or export "intoxicating liquors" for "beverage purposes." Thus, selling alcohol was illegal, but buying it was not. The Volstead Act defined "intoxicating liquors" as any beverage with more than 0.5 percent alcohol content, which allowed low-alcohol "near beer" to be sold legally. Also, industrial alcohol that was not intended for "beverage purposes" was legal, though permits were required to manufacture it.

The Volstead Act also allowed high-percentage beverage alcohol under certain conditions. Sacramental wines, such as those used by devout Jews, were permissible, but regulations were put in place to control their sale. Alcohol could also be acquired with a doctor's prescription, with certain time and volume limitations.

Neither the amendment nor the law specifically prohibited the drinking of alcohol. This had ramifications in regard to personal consumption:

booze at home must go," Wheeler demanded. "Liquor is a menace to patriotism because it puts beer before country."

The Eighteenth Amendment

Having elected additional dry congressmen to office in 1916, and with anti-German sentiments working to its advantage, the ASL was nearing the peak of its power. When President Woodrow Wilson's wartime measures came before Congress in the summer of 1917, the drys tacked on a provision to the Food Control Bill. It prohibited the use of foodstuffs for the manufacture of distilled spirits, which brought liquor manufacturing to a halt. They

- A person could possess and drink alcohol in his or her home. Those who stockpiled booze at their residence before Prohibition took effect and only consumed it there violated no laws.

- It was illegal to store alcohol in some place other than a residence, however. (This point was clarified just days before Prohibition took effect. A mad scramble ensued as people had to move large stockpiles from storage buildings to their homes.)

- It was against the law to make beverages that had more than 0.5 percent alcohol, even for personal use. Home manufacturing became very popular, but it was illegal—with one notable exception:

- The Volstead Act allowed the manufacture of cider and fruit juices for personal consumption. Both will ferment into alcoholic beverages of their own accord, though this was not discussed in the act. Thus, homemade wine and hard cider were legal. This provision was included mostly to appease farmers, who had a long tradition of making hard cider. It was viewed as more proof that drys targeted drinking in the cities while ignoring alcohol use in the country. In practice, plenty of city dwellers made use of the exemption, especially immigrants who had previous experience with winemaking.

then turned their attention to the constitutional amendment that had been languishing for three years.

The attitude of Congress toward Prohibition had changed significantly since the amendment had first been voted on. There were more dry legislators, and some of those who had voted against Prohibition in 1914 had changed their minds on the issue because of the war. The drys felt they had the votes to pass the amendment, but they had to do a little horse trading to overcome procedural obstacles in the Senate. Wets refused to let the bill come up for a vote until a time limit was included: the states would have just six years to ratify the amendment. If three-quarters—thirty-six of forty-eight states—failed to do so by that time, the amendment would fail. This was a very tight schedule for the amendment process. Most amendments have no expiration date: the Twenty-Seventh Amendment, which governs Congressional salary hikes, was originally proposed on September 25, 1789, but it was not ratified for 203 years, until May 7, 1992.

Senator Morris Sheppard of Texas, a co-sponsor of the original resolution, was unsure whether to accept the time constraints on the Eighteenth Amendment. "Half a dozen years seemed an awfully short time to me," he later admitted. "But I had to take a chance. It was the first time in American history we had ever had a chance to get a dry amendment onto the floor for a vote."

The deal was made, and the Senate vote took place on August 1, 1917. The measure passed 65 to 20, comfortably above the two-thirds majority needed. Four months later, after a congressional recess, it came before the House of Representatives, though some changes had been made to the amendment in the meantime. A compromise between the opposing sides had resulted in a seven-year time limit, rather than six, for ratification. In return, the wets won the concession that if the amendment were added to the Constitution, there would be a one-year grace period between its ratification and implementation.

Some changes were also made to the technical wording of the measure— all of them authored by Wayne Wheeler. Though little attention was paid to these alterations at the time, they later had a profound effect on enforcement efforts. The House approved the altered form of the amendment by a resounding 282 to 128 count. At that point, the only hope for the wets was that the seven-year limit would expire before 36 states formally ratified the Prohibition amendment.

While some drys were anxious about the time limit, others were not. The ASL had proven itself the master of state politics long before it had turned its attention to Washington. Bishop James Cannon Jr., a member of the league's executive committee, confidently predicted that "the amendment will be ratified within two years" (see Cannon biography, p. 103). He was correct. Mississippi became the first state to ratify the Eighteenth Amendment on January 8, 1918, and within thirteen months, thirty-five other states had formally approved the amendment. The last of these states was Nebraska, which approved the measure on January 14, 1919. The stage was thus set for the Eighteenth Amendment to become a part of the U.S. Constitution on January 17, 1920.

More than 30,000 gallons of wine from this Los Angeles winery are flushed into the gutter as national Prohibition goes into effect.

A New Era Dawning

Some Americans began stockpiling alcohol in preparation for the drought, but the price of liquor had skyrocketed with the passage of the amendment. Only those with a lot of expendable income could afford to lay in a large supply before Prohibition began. As the deadline approached, it was expected that January 16—the last day for legal alcohol—would be marked by wild parties, especially in New York City, the country's nightlife capital. Instead, as the *New York Evening Post* reported, "the big farewell failed to materialize." The public seemed to be waiting quietly to see what the age of Prohibition would bring.

What Prohibition brought on its first day were large celebrations by drys all over the country. One of the grandest was presented by evangelist Billy

Sunday, a longtime foe of alcohol and a first-rate showman (see biography on Sunday, p. 134). Sunday presided over a funeral for John Barleycorn (a symbolic figure for alcohol), who was laid to rest in a twenty-foot-long casket. The evangelist then proceeded to describe the glorious new era that was at hand. "The reign of tears is over," he said. "The slums will soon be only a memory. We will turn our prisons into factories and our jails into storehouses and corncribs. Men will walk upright now, women will smile, and the children will laugh. Hell will be forever for rent."

Even as these words were spoken, however, there were indications that prisons might need to fulfill their old function for some time to come. Before Prohibition was twenty-four hours old, trucks transporting bootleg liquor had been seized in two U.S. cities, and illegal stills were discovered in two others. In addition, gangs had robbed large amounts of alcohol from a train car and a government storage facility. One of the most crime-ridden eras in American history had begun.

Chapter Three

THE SUPPLY

—⟨⟨⟩⟩—

"The United States government would have to employ an inspector to every man and woman and child who crosses the ferry from Windsor to Detroit. It would have to line the shore for thirty miles with armed guards to hold up and search every craft that tries to land and then it would not begin to make serious inroads on the operation of the rumrunners."

—*New York Times*, June 25, 1927

The reasons that Prohibition failed are many and complicated, but its failure ultimately stemmed from one basic fact: a large number of people continued to desire alcohol after passage of the Eighteenth Amendment, and they were willing and able to satisfy that desire by illegal means. Prohibition did cause a lot of changes in the way Americans drank, but it did not do the one thing it was intended to do—end alcohol consumption. In fact, alcohol continued to flow from a variety of sources throughout the Prohibition era.

Smuggling Alcohol into America

Prohibition brought an immediate surge in attempts to import alcohol illegally from abroad. Smugglers had successfully brought alcohol into dry areas in the years prior to Prohibition, and they wasted no time in conducting a similar trade across the international border. The difficulty of stopping this traffic soon became very clear. The borders of the United States extend for more than 18,000 miles over a blend of land, ocean, lake, and river features. Illegal alcohol was spirited into the United States across all of these boundary types.

33

Most of the contraband alcohol brought into the United States came from Canada. The two countries share a very long border, but the majority of the smuggling took place across the waterways that separate Michigan from Ontario. It is estimated that 75 percent of all the liquor smuggled during Prohibition came via this route. The most popular location of all was the short run across the Detroit River, between the cities of Windsor, Ontario, and Detroit, Michigan. The latter city was home to the notorious Purple Gang, a crime organization that controlled much of the region's Prohibition-era trade in liquor.

This traffic was aided by Canadian liquor laws. During World War I, Canada had outlawed alcohol nationwide, but at the beginning of 1920, the provinces were given the right to decide their own policies. Only Quebec opted to legalize alcohol, but Canadian laws allowed citizens in other provinces to order an unlimited supply from Quebec retailers, so long as it was for personal consumption. As soon as Prohibition began in the United States, Canadian residents near the borders began ordering huge amounts of booze. In just seven months, 900,000 cases of liquor were shipped to five towns in southeastern Ontario. It is doubtful that much of this was personally consumed. (One woman ordered forty cases and nine barrels of whiskey by herself.) Most was boated across the Detroit River to the United States.

Running the River

The development of smuggling along the Detroit River mirrored events elsewhere. In the beginning, small operators conducted the trade—families or individuals who had access to a boat and a desire to make some money. They loaded fishing craft and rowboats with cases of alcohol and ran them across, making use of the river's marshes and islands for cover. This small-scale shipping continued in winter, when cars drove across the frozen river or across nearby Lake St. Clair. There were even individuals who donned skates and pulled sleds of booze across the ice. All kinds of people were in on the game: According to one estimate, reported in Philip P. Mason's *Rumrunning and the Roaring Twenties*, one out of every four residents in Windsor, Ontario, was involved in smuggling in 1920.

These small-scale operations proved short-lived, however. By 1923 organized criminal gangs had taken over the trade. They brought a more sophisticated approach to transporting the goods, making use of high-powered boats, elaborate signal systems, and even whiskey-filled torpedo devices that trav-

U.S. customs officials examine steel torpedoes discovered on a rumrunning schooner. Smugglers sometimes towed whiskey-filled torpedoes to customers during the Prohibition era.

eled beneath the surface of the river. They also brought money to bribe officials, developing elaborate payoff systems that allowed them to move large amounts of liquor with little risk of being arrested.

The land border between northern New York State and Quebec became another important route for contraband booze. With no water to cross, the smuggling in this region was carried out by car or truck. Convoys traveling by night could transit the remote towns with little hindrance. Though plenty of regular autos were used, specially designed vehicles were also put into service to better avoid detection. Some employed metal pans suspended beneath the automobile frame to hold the bottles, while others used false seats to con-

A beer-laden truck that fell through the ice on Lake St. Clair during a Canada-to-United States smuggling run.

ceal their cargo. Other lawmakers employed strategies of ingenious simplicity. One enterprising farmer regularly transported his horses to the Canadian side of the border, loaded them with alcohol, and turned them loose. The animals then found their way back to their U.S. home by themselves, bringing the liquor with them.

Rum Row

Smuggling over the open seas by the so-called rumrunners became one of the most famous conduits for alcohol to reach the United States during Prohibition. The majority of this liquor came from foreign-owned islands in the Caribbean and Atlantic. The Bahamas, which are British territory, were one of the largest suppliers. In fact, some shrewd liquor wholesalers from the United States had moved their supplies there before Prohibition took effect. Jamaica, which was another British holding at that time, and the French islands of St. Pierre and Miquelon were also popular embarkation points.

Ship owners operating in these waters legally purchased large volumes of alcohol on these islands, then set sail to a point just outside of the territorial waters of the United States (the boundary varied between three and twelve miles offshore during Prohibition). The most popular sites were off of Long Island and New Jersey—close to the lucrative New York City market. There, they would drop anchor and await the arrival of smaller boats from shore. Because the ships tended to congregate close together, the place where they anchored was referred to as "rum row"—in honor of the rumrunners—though rum was but one of many options for buyers.

The owners of the small boats purchased as much liquor from the large ships as they could carry, then made a run to shore, hoping to avoid the Coast Guard and Prohibition agents. So long as the larger ships stayed outside of the territorial waters of the United States, they technically were not in violation of any U.S. laws. Most of the risk was assumed by the smaller shore boats, which sometimes became involved in chases and shoot-outs with authorities. A larger danger to both the rum-running ships and the shore boats were hijackers who seized boats and robbed them of their liquor and money. Over time, rumrunners and shore smugglers became increasingly well-armed so they could defend themselves against these modern pirates.

The most famous of the rum row captains was William "Bill" McCoy (see biography on McCoy, p. 119). In fact, McCoy claimed to have founded the rum-row approach after giving up the chancier game of taking the cargo ashore himself. Operating out of the Bahamas, McCoy owned a string of ships and developed a reputation for selling high-quality liquor. In fact, his operation may have been the basis for the origin of the phrase "the real McCoy"—a reference to his top-shelf alcohol.

Rum row flourished during the early years of Prohibition, but by the mid-1920s it had been hurt by two developments. First, the United States secured agreements with several foreign countries to search foreign vessels that came within an hour of shore. (Nearly all of the rumrunners sailed under foreign flags because this had previously provided protection from U.S. law while in international waters.) Second, the Coast Guard commissioned more

A fleet of U.S. Coast Guard vessels based out of Detroit.

than 200 patrol craft that focused on intercepting the shore boats as they returned from rum row. Alcohol continued to flow via the ocean route, but smugglers were forced to rely on specially built high-speed boats that could sneak up to shore at night. These were operated by well-financed organized-crime outfits. The era of the independent daredevils hauling liquor to shore in their sea skiffs had come to an end.

U.S. Liquor Supplies

While smugglers were importing alcohol from other countries, there was already a large supply inside the United States—the inventory of the liquor manufacturers. There were legal ways to get to this booze. The Volstead Act—

the law that was passed to enforce the Eighteenth Amendment—allowed liquor to be prescribed by doctors in limited amounts. Originally the limit was one pint per person every ten days, but it was lowered to a half pint in 1921 when the Willis-Campbell Law was enacted. (This measure also prevented doctors from prescribing beer to patients.) Alcohol was considered a useful medicine in the 1920s, so this provision was seen as necessary, but bootleggers exploited the system in various ways.

First, plenty of bogus prescriptions were issued. Patients—some of whom worked with unscrupulous doctors—filled prescriptions, then sold the liquor to a bootlegger. Second, the drugstores that filled the prescriptions could take the alcohol they obtained legally and dilute it, perhaps doubling the total amount of liquid. They used part of this to fill prescriptions and sold the remainder to bootleggers. Finally, clever operators used the prescription system to divert large amounts of alcohol from distillery stocks.

This third avenue was perfected by George Remus, one of the largest bootleggers to operate during Prohibition (see biography on Remus, p. 126). He began his operation by buying up the whiskey certificates issued by distilleries. These certificates (similar to shares of stock) had lost most of their value with the passage of Prohibition, so Remus bought them very cheaply. He eventually became America's largest owner of distilleries, controlling one third of the whiskey in the country. After securing his supply, he founded numerous drug companies to sell medicinal whiskey. The drug companies withdrew liquor from Remus's distilleries, then used various fraudulent means to sell most of it illegally.

Illegal Manufacturing

Rather than devising ways to get at the existing stocks of alcohol, many bootleggers found it easier to make their own supplies. Illegal manufacture of distilled spirits had occurred throughout the history of the United States. (Before Prohibition, such operations had been illegal because the liquor was unlicensed and untaxed—not because the alcohol itself was forbidden.) The number of illegal stills used to make liquor skyrocketed after passage of the Eighteenth Amendment. More than 17,000 were seized by the government in 1925 alone, and this was only a small fraction of those in operation.

Prohibition agents pose with a captured still in Washington, D.C.

Bootleggers used stills to manufacture alcohol in two different ways. The first was to make it "from scratch." A popular way to do this was to mix yeast, corn sugar, and water. This mixture was left to ferment into a low-alcohol mash, which would then be purified into a stronger form of alcohol, or "hooch," in the still. This was essentially the same process that commercial distilleries used to create alcohol, but on a smaller and cruder scale.

The other method was to distill denatured industrial alcohol that was intended for use in manufacturing items such as antifreeze, camera film, and synthetic fabrics. Most forms of denatured alcohol were poisonous by design. Since the early 1900s, the government had required industrial alcohol to be processed so that it could not be consumed. This did not deter Prohibition bootleggers, however. Once they got their hands on denatured alcohol, they re-distilled it to remove the harmful elements.

In certain tragic instances, however, these attempts to remove the harmful elements failed. On these occasions, the liquid retained poisons that caused people to die, go blind, or suffer other permanent disabilities (see

"The Trouble with 'Jake'" sidebar, p. 43). In one particularly bad incident in Philadelphia in 1923, more than 300 people died in one month from poison-laced alcohol. The nationwide death toll in 1927 from deadly alcohol mixtures was 11,700.

As the body count mounted, there was an outcry against the government regulations that placed the denaturing agents in industrial alcohol. During Senate Judiciary Committee hearings in 1926, James A. Reed of Missouri, one of the leading wet congressmen, described the regulations as "enforcing prohibition by poison." Many advocates of Prohibition, however, were unmoved. "The government is under no obligation to furnish people with alcohol that is drinkable when the Constitution prohibits it," Wayne Wheeler said. "The person who drinks this industrial alcohol is a deliberate suicide."

"Near Beer" and Real Beer

Most alcohol that was smuggled and transported over long distances was distilled liquor, simply because it was more efficient and profitable to move a liquid that had a high percentage of alcohol in it. For instance, a case of whiskey might be sold in New York City for $140; a case of beer, which took up roughly the same amount of space in a car or boat, would bring just $25. As a result, the drinking of hard alcohol increased greatly after passage of the Eighteenth Amendment. Beer did not vanish completely, however. One of the wrinkles of the Volstead Act was that it made it easier for bootleggers to meet the demand for beer.

The law prohibited the manufacture or sale of beverages containing more than 0.5 percent alcohol. However, any beverage that contained less than one-half percent of alcohol was allowed. Thus, it was legal to manufacture and sell "near beer," so long as it stayed below the 0.5 limit. To make near beer, however, brewers had to first make regular beer (which has about four percent alcohol), then reduce the alcohol content to one-half percent. As a result, brewers were allowed to have large supplies of real beer at their factories. Government oversight of the process was very lax, so many brewers began to sell their real beer. The authorities were aware the problem existed but did little to stop it. In 1930, the Prohibition Commissioner confessed that "it is just a question of putting a hose in a high-powered beer tank and filling near-beer kegs with the high-powered beer and running it out as near beer. So it is a rather difficult thing to get at."

A captured rumrunner's boat loaded with liquor.

A more complex way of getting around the 0.5 limit was through the creation of "needle beer." In this approach, "speakeasies"—Prohibition-era establishments that sold alcoholic drinks—bought kegs of near beer but then obtained a separate shipment of high-octane distilled alcohol, sometimes from the same place they got the near beer. When a customer ordered a beer, the bartender would inject some of the alcohol into the glass of near beer to give it more kick. This was far from a scientific measurement, however, and the alcohol content could end up being much higher than a normal beer.

Big Profits for Bootleggers

The reason that smugglers and bootleggers sought out every available source of alcohol was that they could make a lot of money by doing so. For example, simply driving a carload of booze from Quebec to New York City could be enormously profitable. According to historian Sean Dennis Cashman's *Prohibition: The Lie of the Land*, a bottle of whiskey could be purchased in Canada for about $4. Once that bottle reached New York, it could be sold

The Trouble with "Jake"

Many scary alcoholic concoctions were consumed during Prohibition, but one of the worst was Jamaica Ginger, better known as "Jake." The legitimate version of Jamaica Ginger was sold by prescription only and was intended to be used in very small amounts—a drop or two mixed into several ounces of water—to cure stomach ailments. But when it became known that Jake had an alcohol content of more than 80 percent, it became a hot item, especially among the poor who could not afford more expensive forms of black-market booze. Bootleg versions became widely available in Kansas, New England, and several southern states. When the entire two-ounce bottle was mixed into a milkshake or a glass of ginger ale, it was said to pack quite a punch. There was more than alcohol in this liquid, though. It also contained tricresyl phosphate, a denaturing agent, which causes nerve damage. Several days after ingesting Jake, drinkers complained of numbness in their fingers. Later, paralysis attacked their feet, and they became crippled, able to walk only with crutches. There was no cure. In the spring of 1930, some 15,000 cases of "jake paralysis" were documented nationwide, with 500 cases in the town of Wichita, Kansas, alone.

for $12. A single large vehicle that could hold about thirty cases could net the smuggler $2,000 or more after expenses.

Other alcohol supplies were just as lucrative. In recounting his experiences in *The Real McCoy*, William McCoy said that he could bank $46,000 in profit from a single successful schooner run between the Bahamas and rum row. McCoy claimed that the captains of the small boats that ran liquor from ship to shore could pocket $3,000 per trip.

Bootleggers that opted to cook up their own alcohol only needed to invest a few hundred dollars to make a high-capacity still capable of producing 50 to 100 gallons of liquor per day. Cashman estimates that each gallon of booze cost about fifty cents to produce and could be sold for $3 or more. Thus, a bootlegger could earn as much as $250 a day after the cost of the still had been paid off.

The larger the volume, the greater the riches. Big operators such as George Remus took in incredible sums of money. Paul Y. Anderson, a reporter who profiled Remus for the St. Louis *Post-Dispatch*, noted that Remus paid, at most, $4 a case for the whiskey he obtained through his distilleries. He sold it for $80 a case, and there were millions of cases to sell. Of course, Remus had a lot of overhead expenses, including transport trucks and a staff of as many as 3,000 people. He also had to pay millions of dollars in bribes. Still, there was plenty left over for the boss. Remus became a multimillionaire before his elaborate scheme fell apart and he landed in prison.

High Cost, Low Quality

A look at the economics of Prohibition shows why the bootleggers could make so much money. When it became illegal, alcohol increased in price. This phenomenon is true of all contraband items, be they illegal drugs or Cuban cigars. Essentially, consumers compensated the bootleggers for the risks they had to take in breaking the law and also for the bribes that the bootleggers had to pay to conduct their business. According to Cashman, these costs made the price of a Prohibition-era drink cost two to ten times more than it had when alcohol was legal.

The retail price was only part of the profit, however. Most liquor was diluted from its original state. Bootleggers who obtained high-quality alcohol almost always watered it down in "cutting plants." These were very common in the big bootlegging centers. The *Detroit News* estimated that there were 150 large cutting plants operating in the city in 1928, and there were probably many small operations, as well. By diluting the booze, a bootlegger might turn one bottle of 80-proof whiskey into two bottles of 40-proof whiskey (though the counterfeit labels would still read 80 proof). Each bottle would sell for at least twice what a single bottle cost before Prohibition. On top of all that, the liquor was completely untaxed and so were the profits that the bootlegger earned.

All of these factors were good for the sellers, but they were bad for the buyers. Those that continued to drink during Prohibition had to pay very high prices for a product that was usually of very poor quality. If they had the misfortune of getting poison liquor they could even die. Given these factors, it stands to reason that alcohol consumption would have plummeted during Prohibition. Instead, it sometimes seemed that Prohibition further whetted the nation's thirst.

Chapter Four
THE THIRST

—◆◆◆—

"The Prohibition Law will be violated—extensively at first, slightly later on; but it will, broadly speaking, be enforced and will result in a nation that knows not alcohol."

—Daniel C. Roper, Commissioner of Internal Revenue, 1920

"Certainly it would be ridiculous for me to deny that liquor is sold in large and small quantities throughout the country, and that practically anyone who possesses simultaneously a thirst and as much as a quarter dollar can partly assuage that thirst."

—Mabel Walker Willebrandt,
former Assistant Attorney General of the United States, 1929

Exactly how much drinking took place during the Prohibition is a matter of debate. Precise figures are impossible to determine because bootleggers kept no records of their transactions. Estimates have been made, but many of them were produced by groups supporting or opposing Prohibition, so they are likely to be biased. A wet group, the Association against the Prohibition Amendment, compared the annual alcohol consumption of 1926—roughly the midpoint of Prohibition—with average yearly intake in the period between 1910 and 1917. They concluded that Americans drank more under Prohibition than they did previously. Other sources suggested that consumption may have dropped in the early 1920s but soon rose to pre-Prohibition levels. Such estimates can be argued endlessly, so it is probably more useful to focus on a reality that is not in dispute: millions of people violated the law by consuming alcohol, and Prohibition failed to reduce drinking in any meaningful way.

Why were so many Americans willing to become lawbreakers? A number of factors came into play, but two top the list. First, a lot of people in the United States enjoyed drinking alcohol. Second, many Americans felt that legislators had no right to deny them this pleasure. Both of these factors are related to the nation's heritage. As discussed previously, alcohol had a long history in America and an even longer one in Europe. It was not easy to convince people that an activity their ancestors had taken part in for centuries was now forbidden.

Also, while the United States has been home to strict moralists (Increase Mather and Justin Edwards, for instance), it has also produced a long line of statesmen who believe that government should have a limited role in people's lives. History shows that many Americans will defy a law they believe is oppressive. The best-known example is the rebellion against British tax laws, which led to U.S. independence. Another is the Whiskey Rebellion of the 1790s, in which citizens defied the government's attempt to interfere with the sale and consumption of alcohol, in that case by imposing new taxes on the commodity.

The Roaring '20s

The American people have displayed a well-documented affinity for rebellion and questioning of authority ever since the United States was founded, but these characteristics have been particularly evident in certain eras. The 1920s was one of those periods. In that decade, society went through a shake-up that was similar to that of the 1960s. As in the 1960s, this rebellion was led by young people who challenged the values of the previous generation. (They even had their own form of rebellious music—jazz—which gave birth to the term "the Jazz Age.")

But the turbulence of the 1920s was also attributable to a wider feeling that the country had entered a new era. Some of this feeling came from the ever-increasing number of automobiles, the ever-larger growth of cities, the ever-quicker pace of life. Also, the country had just been through the First World War, and while it did not experience the widespread destruction of infrastructure and societal institutions that Europe did in that conflict, the American people did experience some of the same feelings of vulnerability and dislocation in the years that followed. The "War to End All Wars" was over, and yet the

Potent Potables

The widespread appeal of mixed-drink cocktails began as a direct result of the passage of the Eighteenth Amendment. In most pre-Prohibition saloons liquor was served "straight"—by itself. In the Prohibition speakeasies, however, mixers became popular because they helped mask the foul taste of the low-quality alcohol. Also, restaurants and other establishments that did not serve their own alcohol sometimes allowed customers to bring their own alcoholic drinks into the premises (usually in a flask—a stylish and popular accessory). To make this practice less conspicuous, many restaurants sold glasses of mix (ginger ale or orange juice, for instance) into which the alcohol could be poured. As a result, several classic cocktails made their first appearance in the 1920s, including the Manhattan and the Rock and Rye. Others, including the mysteriously named Renee and Howard Cocktail, proved less timeless.

1920s were an uneasy period. The establishment of the Communist-Bolshevik government in Russia and growing political unrest in Italy and Germany led many observers to wonder if conditions were ripening for a second world war.

But along with the uncertainty, there was a sense of possibility. Much of this feeling was fed by the booming economy—at least until 1929, when overvalued stocks came crashing to earth. Before the crash, a lot of people had a lot of money. This affluence had a big effect on those who defied Prohibition. First of all, more people could afford the inflated booze prices. Also, because the many wealthy Americans continued to drink as much as they pleased during Prohibition, drinking became trendy. In *The Theory of the Leisure Class*, Thorstein Veblen notes that alcohol often becomes a sign "of the superior status of those who could afford the indulgence." The "smart set" of the 1920s was pictured as well-dressed men and women sipping cocktails. Nothing conveyed social rank better than the places where the sipping took place.

Speakeasies

Before Prohibition, Americans had done more of their drinking in public than in private. That tradition did not end in 1920, but it did undergo a major

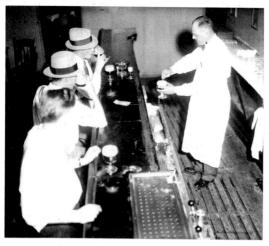

Customers belly up to the bar at a Detroit blind pig, also known as a speakeasy.

change. The saloon—at least in its old form—was no more. If nothing else, the drys could take pride in the fact that the sordid, smelly drinking spots that had openly offended the dignity of America's main streets had disappeared. Unfortunately for the drys, the end of the saloon did not spell the end of the drinking establishment. The 1920s became the era of the speakeasy—the illegal barroom.

Speakeasies had been around long before Prohibition. As long as there had been liquor license laws, there were places that violated those laws and operated illegally. Speakeasies had actually become rather familiar just prior to Prohibition, because a large number had sprung up in the dry areas created by local-option and state laws in the 1900s and 1910s.

During Prohibition, however, their numbers exploded. New York City was estimated to contain 5,000 speakeasies in 1922, and the number grew dramatically in the following years. In 1929 the police commissioner put the New York total at 32,000, which, if correct, would have been twice the number of drinking spots that existed in the city before Prohibition.

Similar trends evolved throughout the country. In testimony before the Senate Judiciary Committee in 1926, Judge Alfred J. Talley maintained that nationwide there were three speakeasies operating for each pre-Prohibition saloon. The *Detroit News* estimated that Detroit was home to between 16,000 and 25,000 illegal establishments in 1928. One local reporter put it in less statistical terms: "It was absolutely impossible to get a drink in Detroit," he wrote, "unless you walked at least ten feet and told the busy bartender what you wanted in a voice loud enough for him to hear you above the uproar." The only positive news for the drys in this regard was that the number of illegal bars decreased somewhat after the stock-market crash of 1929—largely because people had less money to spend.

Speakeasies came in all shapes and sizes, but they shared some common features. Not wishing to attract attention to themselves, they avoided prominent locations and had no signs to advertise their presence. They were frequently located in residential buildings rather than retail storefronts or office buildings. In New York, the brownstone houses were favorite places for the more expensive speakeasies. Some establishments left their doors open for anyone to enter, though most barrooms that operated in this manner had very good "protection": in other words, they paid large bribes to the proper authorities to ensure that their employees and guests would not face arrest. More commonly, the doors to the speakeasy were kept locked. Patrons had to ring a doorbell and were given a good looking over before being admitted. In some cases, newcomers were only admitted if they knew a certain password or were accompanied by a regular customer that would vouch for them.

The High Life

Beyond their common need for secrecy, speakeasies varied widely in their characteristics. The ones that have lived on in the public imagination are the exclusive, high-class establishments that served a well-heeled clientele. Such places were found primarily in large cities such as New York and Chicago. In a passage from Studs Terkel's *Hard Times*, Alec Wilder fondly remembered the New York City establishments he frequented during Prohibition:

> As soon as you walked in the door, you were a special person, you belonged to a special society. When I'd bring a person in, it was like dispensing largesse. I was a big man. You had to know somebody who knew somebody. It had that marvelous movie-like quality, unreality. And the food was great.

Wilder's opinion of the food was a rare one. Most people felt that even the expensive speakeasies served mediocre food, if they served any at all. But many high-end spots did offer more than a place to hunker down with a drink: they offered entertainment. It was during Prohibition that the nightclub came into its own. The clubs of New York City reigned supreme. Duke Ellington, Fred Astaire, Jimmy Durante, and other show-business legends got their start in Prohibition-era speakeasies such as the Cotton Club and the Trocadero. Some nightspots offered more unusual amusements. The opulent Country Club boasted ping-pong tables and a miniature-golf course but was probably better known for its proprietor, Belle Livingstone, who supervised

Patrons and bartenders are serenaded by an orchestra (not seen) at this drinking haven in New York.

the club while attired in red lounging pajamas. "Texas" Guinan, a former vaudeville performer and movie actress, was another famed female club manager. Decked out in furs and diamonds, she cajoled her patrons with shouts of "Hello, sucker!," which became a catch phrase for the era.

At the opposite end of the spectrum were crude places far removed from the glamour that many associate with the 1920s. "All you need is two bottles and a room and you have a speakeasy," commented New York City Police Commissioner Grover A. Whalen. This was an accurate description of many of the no-frills joints that clung to life during the Prohibition era. Such places were more likely to serve alcohol that was of poor or even dangerous quality, partly because owners could not afford anything better and partly because the clientele did not have the economic power to demand a better product. In testimony before the National Commission on Law Observance and Enforcement, John Van Vaerenewyck described a low-end speakeasy and the "refreshments" it served:

> You get into a room where they are selling this stuff. The doors
> are barred or locked. You will sit around the table with a group
> of men—4 or 5 or 6, or probably 50. You sit around the table
> and you have this stuff shelled out to you. It is 50 cents a drink
> in most places. After the third drink your brain ... is immedi-
> ately a muddle. You can feel that stuff going through your
> whole system because it is raw. The fusel oil [a byproduct of
> the distillation process] has not been taken out to any large
> degree.... . Your stomach begins to turn.... . Everybody is talk-
> ing silly and acting foolish and singing songs or anything else.

Like their high-dollar cousins, the low-rent watering holes were often located in residences, but in some cases families were still residing there. "They are a terrible menace as they have brought the sale of liquor into tene- ment and dwelling houses, and within the purview of children," Judge Talley said of such speakeasies. "Terrible fights are common in them, provoked by the raw liquor they sell and unavoidable absence of police supervision." A Croatian immigrant from Cleveland, quoted in Martha Bruére's *Does Prohibi- tion Work*, made a similar complaint: "Now wine and whisky sold in homes. No good for woman to stay and sell liquor to mens all day. They get drunk and say bad things before children and she forget husband and children. Saloons was better; no children could go there and no women."

Equal Opportunity

But the women *were* present—and not just in the low-end dives. With the advent of Prohibition, females rich and poor joined men in public drink- ing. This was the most striking difference between the saloon and the speakeasy. Before Prohibition the only women seen near a barroom were prostitutes or anti-alcohol protestors. Now they were customers.

The reason for this dramatic change has been debated, but it was likely due to a combination of factors. Prohibition arrived in a time when women were achieving a greater public role after decades of struggle: the Nineteenth Amendment, which gave women throughout the U.S. the right to vote, had

A woman shows off a miniature alcohol flask that tucks into her garter.

passed in 1920. Also, women's behavior was part of the larger social upheaval of the 1920s. Free-living, cocktail-sipping young women (dubbed "flappers" by the press) were one more sign that the old rules no longer applied.

Of course, when it came to alcohol, the old rules *did not* apply: the admittance of women into the barrooms was eased by the fact that neither the speakeasy owners nor the male customers wanted to create a fuss that would draw attention to their illegal activity. Finally, though it has never been proven by a careful study, it is possible that men accepted women in the speakeasies simply because they came to enjoy their company. Bars suddenly became places to meet and woo the opposite sex—much as they are today—and some men saw that as a good thing. Among them was Alec Wilder, who conveyed his feelings in Studs Turkel's *Hard Times*. "The speaks were so romantic," Wilder said. "A pretty girl in a speak-easy was the most beautiful girl in the world."

Home Drinking and Home Brewing

The high cost of alcohol also encouraged more drinking at homes than had occurred in the pre-Prohibition era. Bootleggers supplied the home drinker as well as the barrooms, and some developed delivery systems for these transactions. In addition, retail stores sometimes sold liquor along with their other goods. Famed Prohibition agent Izzy Einstein once encountered a grocery in Harlem that sold its liquor by a system of code words: "a small can of beans" was a pint of whiskey; "a small can of tomatoes" was a pint of gin. A "large can" of either was a quart bottle.

Many home drinkers made the alcohol they consumed themselves. In fact, beer-, wine-, and liquor-making became popular hobbies for countless Americans. The Volstead Act provided a loophole for some of this activity. It

Authorities dismantle a still in San Francisco.

allowed the manufacture of fruit juices and ciders for home use, even though the juice could be easily turned into an alcoholic beverage just by setting it aside for an extended period. Grape growers, whose business had been threatened by the ban on wine, quickly figured out a new way to market their produce. They produced bricks of grape concentrate that could be dissolved in water to make "fruit juice" that had non-juicy names such as sherry and burgundy. Manufacturers also packaged their product with labels that assured buyers that the contents would ferment and turn into wine. These "warning" labels proved a significant boon to sales. Beer-making supplies such as malt syrup and wort were also widely available, as were small stills for distilling liquor.

It was not illegal to sell such items. The law breaking only began when they were used to make alcohol. But there were very few arrests for home manufacturing: it was so widespread it was almost impossible to police.

Besides, law enforcement agencies had plenty of large-scale alcohol peddlers to pursue. Unfortunately, it would prove more or less impossible to stop them, too.

Chapter Five
THE ENFORCERS

"This law will be obeyed in cities, large and small, and where it is not obeyed it will be enforced…. The law says that liquor to be used as a beverage must not be manufactured. We shall see that it is not manufactured. Nor sold, nor given away, nor hauled in anything on the surface of the earth, or in the air."

—John F. Kramer, Prohibition Commissioner

"In order to enforce prohibition, it will require a police force of 250,000 men and a force of 250,000 men to police the police."

—Congressman Fiorello La Guardia
on conditions in New York City

While the Eighteenth Amendment provided the constitutional basis for prohibiting alcohol, it—like most amendments—did not address the details of how Prohibition would be accomplished. Instead, it was up to Congress to enact the precise laws related to alcohol enforcement. Congress responded by passing the Volstead Act in October 1919, overriding President Wilson's veto. Officially known as the National Prohibition Enforcement Act, its more popular name came from Congressman Andrew Volstead, who introduced the legislation in the House of Representatives. But while Volstead sponsored the bill, it was actually written by Wayne Wheeler of the Anti-Saloon League.

The Volstead Act attempted to lay the foundation for the execution of an enormous task. As the National Commission on Law Observance and

Enforcement (better known as the Wickersham Commission) later noted, Prohibition required "total abstinence on the part of 122,000,000 people who had been accustomed to consume 2,000,000 gallons of alcoholic beverages per annum." With regard to regulating personal conduct, the act was the most sweeping legal change ever attempted in the United States.

Graft and Corruption in Enforcement Agencies

Prohibition's ultimate failure stemmed in part from the shortcomings of the federal agency that was created for the express purpose of enforcing the nation's alcohol statutes. The Prohibition Unit (its name was changed to the Prohibition Bureau in 1927) was made up of just over 1,500 agents when it was first created. The agency grew larger in the years that followed, but never exceeded 3,000 agents in the field. The agency was aided by local and state police agencies, the U.S. Coast Guard, and customs officials, but the Prohibition Unit served as the primary line of defense against the illegal sale and consumption of alcohol. As time passed, it became clear that the resources of the agency were completely inadequate to tackle the challenge before it.

This situation was made worse by the poor quality of some of the men who became Prohibition agents. This problem stemmed from the way that Wayne Wheeler had written the Volstead Act. In order to win wider support for the bill, Wheeler had exempted the Prohibition Unit from Civil Service hiring guidelines, which allowed politicians to use the agency as a means of political patronage. In other words, they rewarded their supporters by handing them government jobs in the Prohibition Unit—a practice that was illegal in most federal departments. As a result, numerous men of questionable talent and motivation received enforcement jobs.

This state of affairs clearly rankled those enforcement officials who were genuinely concerned about enforcing Prohibition. For example, Major Chester P. Mills, the Prohibition Administrator of New York City, angrily told *Collier's Magazine* in 1927 that the hiring practices amounted to nothing more than a "party-spoils system" that created an environment in which "three-quarters of the twenty-five hundred dry agents are ward heelers [workers for political machines] and sycophants named by the politicians."

Those men who joined the Prohibition Unit were not lured by high official salaries. In 1920, a Prohibition agent earned between $1,200 and $2,000 annu-

Detroit police with liquor and stills confiscated in a raid.

ally. This was not lucrative pay, given that the U.S. Bureau of Labor estimated that the average family of five people needed $1,920 per year to survive in the mid-1920s. Why, then, did the agents take the jobs? Some did so because they planned to supplement their salary with bribe money. Bootleggers were always looking to pay off enforcement officials so that they could operate without fear of arrest. According to one estimate, an agent on the take could collect as much as $50,000 per year. In his book *Prohibition Inside Out*, Roy A. Haynes, the second Prohibition commissioner, confessed that some members of his unit considered the agent's badge as "nothing but a license to make money."

Not every agent was crooked, and many of those who joined the force probably had good intentions at the outset. But the temptations were tremendous. Agents were paid barely enough to live on, yet they were expected to honestly police a trade where thousands of dollars could be earned for a few hours' work. The situation was even worse for customs officials and state and local police, who often made less than the Prohibition agents did. The outcome was predictable. A large number of officials and law enforcement officers accepted payoffs and allowed the alcohol to flow.

Looking the Other Way

The enforcement problem made itself known almost immediately. Just ten days after Prohibition took effect, two Chicago agents were charged with accepting bribes from a bootlegger. From that time until the Eighteenth Amendment was repealed thirteen years later, bribery was rampant and took many forms. In Detroit, bootleggers arranged group payoffs to the officers who patrolled the Detroit River in boats. In return, the policemen all called in sick on a predetermined date, giving the smugglers a "free night" to run the river. In *The Real McCoy*, Bill McCoy recalled a similar set-up on his first rum-running voyage. While unloading cases of contraband booze along the Georgia coast, McCoy spotted a patrol boat closing in on his ship. The man who had hired McCoy simply told him, "I got them fixed." Sure enough, the patrol boat passed by as if the rum-running ship did not exist.

This relatively simple form of corruption was known as "looking the other way": law-enforcement officers let the bootleggers go about their business and pretended not to notice their illegal activities. Some agents and police became more actively involved in the alcohol traffic. Some re-sold alcohol they had seized from bootleggers. Others even provided police escorts for bootleggers' shipments to make sure they arrived at their destination without any problems.

Prohibition Bureau records reveal that between 1920 and 1931, almost 9 percent of the agency's personnel were dismissed for corrupt practices. It is likely that there were many other crooked agents who were never found out, or whose offenses were deemed too inconsequential for dismissal. The situation was made worse because other law enforcement agencies—city police, state police, customs officers, and others—also accepted bribes, though records tracking incidence of these types of graft were not maintained.

Some of the bribe-takers brazenly flaunted their new-found wealth. Stories proliferated of officers who began reporting to work in chauffeured limousines and wearing expensive clothes and jewelry. This state of affairs prompted the superintendent of the New Jersey Anti-Saloon League to remark sarcastically that "I don't know of anyone who can make a dollar go further than policemen and dry agents. By frugality, after a year in the service, they acquire automobiles and diamonds."

High-level Corruption

The corruption extended to senior-level officials, as well. One infamous case involved William McConnell, who served as Prohibition director for the state of Pennsylvania. In 1921, an assistant U.S. attorney found proof that McConnell had conspired to remove illegally 700,000 gallons of alcohol from storage. The U.S. attorney also uncovered evidence that McConnell presided over a $4 million slush fund used to bribe various Prohibition agents and officials.

The dishonesty could go even higher. United States Attorney General Harry M. Daugherty, a close confidant of President Warren G. Harding, became implicated in

Harry Daugherty, who served as U.S. attorney general from 1921 to 1924.

corrupt activity related to alcohol during the three years (1921-1924) he spent in office. Most of this activity was coordinated through Jess Smith, Daugherty's aide and Harding's former campaign manager.

The most damaging details about Smith and Daugherty came from bootlegging kingpin George Remus after his conviction and imprisonment. In testimony before a Senate committee, Remus stated that he had paid Smith large sums of money to avoid punishment for his bootlegging activities. The payments were as much as $50,000 at a time and totaled in the hundreds of thousands of dollars. In return for these sums, Smith assured Remus that he would be protected from prosecution. Even after the bootlegger was initially found guilty, Smith insisted that the conviction would be overturned because of Smith's "friendship with the general" (Attorney General Daugherty). Smith committed suicide in 1923, possibly because he was about to be indicted for his activities. Daugherty was forced to resign in 1924 but never faced charges—he had protected himself by leaving the actual money handling to Smith.

Remus's activities showed how elaborate the payoff system could become. Though he owned large supplies of whiskey, he often had to arrange for permits to withdraw the alcohol from warehouses. This cost him about $3,000 per permit, and that was just the beginning of the handouts. Small amounts of money and booze were supplied to policemen who patrolled the area near Remus's storage and bottling facilities. More money went to police detectives in Cincinnati, his base of operations, to ensure that delivery trucks could make their rounds without problems. (Some of the detectives even served as sales agents.) Payments were also made to agents from the Prohibition Unit and to police officials in other regions of the country where Remus's network operated.

The bootlegger claimed that bribery expenses devoured fully half of the money he took in from his operation, though some scholars are skeptical of this estimate. John Kobler, for example, estimated in *Ardent Spirits* that 25 percent was a more accurate figure. At any rate, Remus handed out tens of millions of dollars in payments, and the bootlegger claimed that only two officials ever turned down his offers. "I tried to corner the graft market," Remus told the St. Louis *Post-Dispatch*, "but I learnt that there isn't enough money in the world to buy up all the public officials that demand their share of it."

The Real "Untouchables"

Some agents refused to be corrupted. The downfall of George Remus began with the two men he was unable to "fix": Sam Collins, the Prohibition director of Kentucky, and Burt Morgan, the Prohibition director of Indiana. Working together, they engineered a raid on Remus's headquarters near Cincinnati. As a result, the bootlegger was sentenced to the first of his jail terms in 1922. Remus claimed to have offered both men hundreds of thousands of dollars to leave his operation alone. Both refused, despite the fact that they were earning annual salaries of just $4,600.

Honest officials such as Collins and Morgan became known as "untouchables" because they could not be "touched," or corrupted. The term was

Authorities unload bootleg liquor from a confiscated airplane.

later applied most famously to a group of Prohibition agents headed by Eliot Ness, who targeted mobster Al Capone in Chicago. Their contribution to Capone's downfall was modest, however. The exploits later attributed to Ness and his fellow agents in the *Untouchables* television series and feature film were largely fictional.

There were also honest and effective administrators in the Justice Department. One was Mabel Walker Willebrandt, who served as assistant attorney general from 1921 to 1929 (see biography on Willebrandt, p. 141). Willebrandt was a maverick, first because she was a high-ranking woman at a time when men dominated the legal profession, but also because she was an outspoken supporter of Prohibition who backed her words with strong action. She successfully prosecuted some of the biggest bootleggers in the country, including Roy Olmstead, a smuggling kingpin in Washington state, and George Remus.

Willebrandt was unafraid to criticize those elements of the Prohibition effort that she believed were lacking. She found many Prohibition agents to be "as devoid of honesty and integrity as the bootlegging fraternity," and she was an outspoken opponent of politicians who interfered with the duties of prosecutors and agents. Her commitment to strict enforcement of the Volstead Act is expressed in her book *The Inside of Prohibition* (see "Mabel Walker Willebrandt on Enforcement and Politics" sidebar, p. 64).

While Willebrandt garnered a lot of press, the most famous person involved in enforcing Prohibition was an unassuming, portly man who went to work as a Prohibition agent in New York City. Isidor "Izzy" Einstein had no previous law-enforcement experience when he applied for a job with the newly created Prohibition Unit in 1920. The supervisor was not impressed with him or his credentials, but Izzy was persistent. "I insisted that even though I had no gumshoe experience to offer, I *did* know something about *people*—their ways and habits—how to mix with them and gain their confidence," Einstein recalled in his memoir, *Prohibition Agent No. 1*. Once he won the job, Izzy put that knowledge to work—along with a skill he had not told his boss about: an ability to act.

Einstein's job involved searching out speakeasies and getting them to sell him alcohol so that he could make an arrest. He outfitted himself in costumes so that he would not arouse suspicion, posing as a peddler, a cigar salesman, a football player, a ditch-digger, a rich socialite, and numerous other roles. His get-ups and his convincing performances fooled thousands of bartenders and waiters. In his five-year career as an agent, he apprehended nearly 5,000 people and was involved in 20 percent of the arrests in the Lower New York District. On many occasions, Einstein was accompanied by Moe Smith, a fellow agent, who co-starred with Izzy in a variety of sting operations. The agents' success and their amusing costumes made for good newspaper copy, and "Izzy and Moe" eventually became well-known figures throughout the country.

In the end, Izzy became too successful for his own good. "Maybe I trod on toes that were supposed to be protected," he wrote. "My activity and my results didn't make the records of some of the other agents look any too good. Consequently there was hard feeling." After refusing a transfer to Chicago, his job was terminated during a reorganization of the department. Moe Smith was let go at the same time. The dismissal of Einstein and Smith—two of the most honest, hardworking, and popular law-enforcement agents in the country—came in November 1925, a time when Prohibition was in full retreat.

Prohibition agents Isadore "Izzy" Einstein, left, and Moe Smith.

Dangerous Work, Dangerous Workers

While the public loved the antics of Izzy and Moe, many Prohibition agents were widely disliked and their behavior was often criticized, especially in large metropolitan areas were Prohibition was most unpopular. The biggest complaint—aside from corruption—was that the agents posed a danger to the public. They were frequently involved in shooting incidents. According to the Wickersham Commission, 144 people died in encounters with Prohibition agents between 1920 and 1931, though other sources put the total closer to 200. These figures do not include alcohol-related shootings by local and state officers, which were common though not well documented. To some degree, gunplay was expected: the agents were often trying to apprehend well-armed criminals who did not hesitate to use their own firearms. Indeed,

63

Mabel Walker Willebrandt on Enforcement and Politics

Assistant Attorney General Mabel Walker Willebrandt was one of the leading Prohibition figures in the Justice Department during the 1920s. Throughout her tenure, she displayed little patience with those who criticized or violated the nation's Prohibition laws. In her 1929 book *The Inside of Prohibition*, she defended her strong law-and-order approach:

> You can neither coax, scold nor nag people into law observance. Consequently, *enforcement* is the necessary approach at this time. Enforcement in court, not promises. Orderly enforcement. Strictly legal methods of enforcement. Enforcement by trained, highly intelligent men, imbued with high morale and a pride in their service. Courageous enforcement. Enforcement backed up at Washington. Everybody would not like such enforcement, but everybody would respect it—even politicians.
>
> Politics has said: Enforcement can't be orderly and unremitting because it must be periodically relaxed when we need the underworld vote. It must not even be strong as the law generally is in a place like New York, where

sixty agents were killed in the line of duty between 1920 and 1931, according to the Wickersham Commission.

Not all of the shooting incidents were so clear-cut and justified, however. Innocent and unarmed civilians were sometimes killed because they were mistaken as bootleggers. Accidental shootings also took place, often when an agent fired what was supposed to be a warning shot only to have it strike someone by mistake. The frequency of such incidents alarmed many people. When combined with the number of people killed or wounded by bootleggers, these shootings added to the sense that Prohibition had made the country more dangerous. "What the prohibition situation needs, first of all, is disarmament," wrote social activist Jane Addams in a 1929 issue of *Survey Graphic*. "The federal agents should be taught some other methods than those of the gunmen."

people are "touchy" on the subject. We must appoint not trained men but those who get the vote out and who will be reasonable with the boys.

Evasive politicians from districts where the dry sentiment is very strong, in order to capture the dry vote at approaching elections, often urge the headquarters to issue "Pollyanna" statements of how many agents will be rushed into that quarter and how effective prohibition is *going to be* to-morrow—always to-morrow! But when some agent or attorney actually does act with courage, old "Political Pull," in the form of some officeholder or committeeman, sidles into offices at Washington and influences some puerile "higher-up" to issue a vacilating statement or apology and to transfer that agent to Arizona or Kansas! No wonder at such times courageous men on the fighting line lose their morale!

But one battle after another to try a case or improve personnel has made me know that worth-while results can be obtained, even in the constant warfare against politics, by grit, persistence and organization.

Gunplay was just one of the reasons that agents were disliked. A bigger reason, at least in areas that had never had much dry support, was simply that the agents were enforcing a very unpopular law. One such place was New Jersey, which had strongly opposed Prohibition. Colonel Ira L. Reeves, the state's Prohibition commissioner, testified to the unpopularity of his men. "I do not know of a single agent on my force," he said, "who was accepted by the community in which he lived as a welcome neighbor and citizen in whom people could place confidence."

Prohibition Cases Clog the Courts

As the Prohibition era moved forward, the sheer number of people charged with violating the alcohol statutes clogged the courts, with the worst backups taking place in the federal courts. Congress had made no provision for increasing the number of courts or prosecutors, apparently believing that the laws would be widely obeyed. When it became clear that this confidence was misplaced, various agencies began trumpeting the need for additional investment in the federal court system. The 1924 annual report of the Department of Justice, for example, declared that "the United States courts today are staggering under the load imposed on them by prohibition legislation."

Even when the scope of the violations became clear, however, no increase in judicial funding was forthcoming. The logjam eased only after judges began imposing special programs to speed things along. They established innovative programs such as so-called "bargain days," in which people accused of alcohol violations were allowed to plead guilty with the understanding that they would be sentenced to small fines, usually $100 or less.

Even when these special bargains were not offered, the punishments dictated in the Volstead Act did little to deter alcohol violations. When Prohibition was first implemented, lawbreakers were charged with misdemeanors. On a first conviction, they faced a maximum fine of $1,000 or six months in jail. Subsequent violations could result in a $2,000 fine and as much as five years in jail.

In 1929, the Jones Act upped the penalties. Violations were classified as felonies and a first conviction could result in a fine of $10,000 or five years in jail. Such sentences were tough, but the maximum terms were seldom imposed. The accused usually worked out some type of plea bargain. In 1931, the average fine was still less than $250.

Enforcement Efforts Starved for Funding

Enforcement efforts were also hampered by state budgets, most of which failed to allocate much funding for Prohibition enforcement activities. The Eighteenth Amendment included a passage that stated "the Congress and the several states shall have concurrent power to enforce this article by appropriate legislation." This was one of the revisions inserted by Wayne Wheeler after passage by the Senate. Wheeler may have added the phrase because he wanted to help convince reluctant states that they would have some say in the question of Prohibition, but it ended up muddying the waters when it came to enforcing the law. States that were lukewarm about Prohibition interpreted the phrase to mean that they *could* enforce the alcohol statutes but that they were not required to do so.

A truck full of confiscated liquor awaiting destruction.

Consequently, many states put little or no money toward enforcement. In 1927, the forty-eight states combined spent about $548,000 in combating alcohol traffic, a paltry percentage of their overall budgets. As Sean Dennis Cashman points out in *Prohibition: The Lie of the Land*, the states spent eight times more money on enforcing their fish and game laws than they did on enforcing the Prohibition statutes. Even state governments that strongly supported Prohibition were reluctant to commit financial resources to enforcing its provisions. These states felt that the enforcement of Prohibition was a federal responsibility because it had been created by a federal amendment.

All parties recognized that if the Prohibition enforcement agencies were going to make any kind of real impact on the alcohol trade, they needed more funding to hire additional personnel and to compensate them at a level that would make them less vulnerable to bribery and graft. Similarly, if local and state police officers were going to be of much help in the Prohibition crusade, more state funds needed to go to them. And if the courts were going to prosecute the thousands of Prohibition-related alcohol cases brought before them in a timely manner, greater investment in the legal system was essential. In other words, someone needed to pay the bill if Prohibition was going to be enforced effectively.

The U.S. Congress, however, shrank from making the tough choices necessary to increase funding, even though drys had almost a three-to-one advantage over the wets in both the House and Senate in the mid-1920s. Likewise, Presidents Warren G. Harding and Calvin Coolidge made no effort to push a stricter enforcement program (see biography on Harding, p. 111).

There was a very practical reason why lawmakers remained so passive about Prohibition's difficulties: It would have been politically dangerous to enforce Prohibition. To devote more funds to stopping the illegal alcohol trade, lawmakers would have to increase taxes or decrease spending on other popular services. They had no stomach for doing either, especially for the sake of an amendment that was already unpopular with a sizable number of voters. When it came to alcohol, elected representatives spent a lot of time talking about law and order, but they refused to pay for it.

Chapter Six

THE MOB

⚊⚍⚍⚍⚍⚍⚍⚊

"If I break the law, my customers, who number hundreds of the best people in Chicago, are as guilty as I am. The only difference is between us is that I sell and they buy. Everybody calls me a racketeer. I call myself a business man. When I sell liquor, it's bootlegging. When my patron serves it on a silver tray on Lake Shore Drive, it's hospitality."

—Al Capone

Organized crime and Prohibition were made for one another. In his book *The American Mafia*, Joseph L. Albini notes that in the United States, criminal syndicates "have existed only as a means of providing illicit goods and services." Thanks to Prohibition, an extremely popular substance—alcohol—became one of these illicit goods, providing organized criminals with more income and power than they had ever had before. To understand how the criminal gangs operated during Prohibition, there's no better place to look than the city that became synonymous with mobsters and machine guns in the 1920s: Chicago.

Organizing the Criminals

Prior to Prohibition, the criminal gangs of Chicago specialized in other illegal services, primarily gambling and prostitution. When Prohibition began, an Italian immigrant named "Big Jim" Colosimo was the most powerful figure in the Chicago underworld, operating a chain of popular "roadhouse" resorts in small towns surrounding Chicago. He was assisted by his wife's nephew,

Mobster Johnny Torrio (center) was an underworld mentor to Al Capone.

Johnny Torrio. Big Jim failed to appreciate the opportunity that Prohibition presented—partly because he was distracted by a new woman in his life, a young, aspiring opera singer named Dale Winter. Johnny Torrio, on the other hand, recognized the fortune that could be made in alcohol, and in the early months of 1920 he urged Colosimo to take action.

Big Jim hesitated. He had other things to think about. In March he divorced his wife, and three weeks later he married Winter. "This is the real thing," he said, when he told Torrio of his new love. "It's your funeral," Torrio replied. Shortly after returning from his honeymoon, Big Jim was gunned down in the lobby of a restaurant he owned. Though the murder was never solved, most experts believe that Torrio ordered the killing so that he could move into bootlegging in a big way.

In addition to the Colosimo-Torrio operation, several other Chicago-based criminal syndicates rushed to carve out a share of the lucrative alcohol business for themselves. Early on, Torrio recognized that the best way to maximize profit and avoid problems was to divide the city between these powerful gangs. In this strategy Torrio was similar to business titans such as J. P. Morgan. These business leaders felt that competition was a bad thing because it endangered profit. In Torrio's case, it also endangered lives, because the gangs usually settled matters with guns. A skilled diplomat, Torrio convinced the other mob bosses that cooperation was the road to riches, and their uneasy alliance held from 1920 to early 1923. The plan was aided by Chicago mayor "Big Bill" Thompson. Notoriously corrupt, Thompson's administration allowed the gangsters to buy complete protection from prosecution. Distilleries ran around the clock, making no effort to disguise their activities, and fleets of beer trucks traveled regular routes with no fear of arrest.

In 1923 Thompson decided not to seek re-election because he faced almost certain defeat. When William Dever became the new mayor of Chicago, he proved less compliant than his predecessor. Determined to enforce

Prohibition laws, he worked to dismantle the corrupt relationship between city hall and the criminal syndicates. Police protection arrangements were thrown into chaos, and the mayor began closing many of the "soft-drink parlors" that served as thinly disguised speakeasies. Intent on offsetting these sudden losses of income, gangs made brazen incursions into one another's territory. Predictably, these forays were met with violence. With the age of diplomacy over, Torrio invested more authority in a trusted

Chicago Mayor William Hale Thompson.

lieutenant who was known for ruthless action. His name was Al Capone (see biography on Capone, p. 107).

Of the various outfits involved in Chicago bootlegging, two had emerged as rivals to the Torrio/Capone organization. The first was the so-called Terrible Gennas, a group of Sicilian brothers who specialized in distilling industrial liquor. The other was the North Side Gang, a mix of Irish, Polish, Jewish, and Italian immigrants headed by Dean O'Banion, a longtime street tough who also had a great love of flowers. He operated his own floral shop on North State Street.

O'Banion proved the most predatory. He hijacked several large shipments belonging to the Gennas, and he masterminded a devious scheme that led to the arrest of Torrio at a Chicago brewery. Because this was Torrio's second alcohol offense, he faced the possibility of jail time. Torrio and the Gennas decided that drastic action was called for.

One day in the fall of 1924 three men walked into O'Banion's flower shop to pick up an arrangement they had ordered for a funeral. O'Banion introduced himself and offered his hand. One of the strangers took it and did not let go. The other two produced pistols and shot the florist down.

Torrio and the Gennas had their revenge, but their triumph proved fleeting. Three months later, Bugs Moran, Hymie Weiss, and another member of the North Side Gang paid a visit to Johnny Torrio. Johnny was shot three times in front of his apartment but managed to survive. The attack marked the end of his days as an active gang leader. A short time later he turned his operation over to Al Capone and retired to Italy (though Torrio would continue to operate behind the scenes). Torrio had always been known for his intelligence. Getting away from the bloody Chicago battles may have been the smartest thing he ever did.

The Beer Wars

From 1925 onward, shootouts, bombings, and assassinations became the order of the day as the rival gangs took aim at one another. Known as the Beer Wars, these battles resulted in hundreds of deaths. Most of the victims were gangsters, though others were sometimes caught in the crossfire. As the killings continued, Capone emerged as the master of the game. Known as "the Big Fella" to underlings and "Scarface" to his enemies, Capone built a well-organized and ruthless operation. He destroyed the formidable Genna syndicate in a matter of weeks. Capone arranged a wave of assassinations that depleted the Genna leadership to the point that survivors fled Chicago entirely.

The North Side Gang proved more of a challenge. In one 1926 assault, the North Siders sent a convoy of cars to attack Capone's headquarters in the Chicago suburb of Cicero. They employed the gangsters' new weapon of choice—the Thompson machine gun, better known as the "tommy gun" or the "Chicago piano." The mobile machine gunners sprayed Capone's building with bullets but failed to kill Capone or anyone else. Capone retaliated one month later. Gunmen stationed in two separate buildings mowed down Hymie Weiss, the leader of the North Siders, as he crossed State Street. When Weiss hit the pavement, he was lying in front of the same flower shop where Dion O'Bannion had died.

Well aware of the dangers of a mob war, Capone took to surrounding himself with a large entourage of well-armed bodyguards. To enhance his safety when he traveled, he had an armor-plated car specially built by General Motors at a cost of $30,000. Despite his well-founded fears of being shot, Capone dressed and lived flamboyantly and frequently appeared in public. Meanwhile, his operation became ever more lucrative. By the late 1920s he was bringing in an estimated $50 million annually. This wealth enabled him to curry favor with Chicagoans devastated by the Stock Market Crash of 1929; he opened soup kitchens all across the city, and paid for the distribution of food and clothing to numerous ailing families.

A line outside one of Capone's Depression-era soup kitchens in Chicago.

In the meantime, the body count continued to rise. From 1926 to 1930, more than 300 mobsters were killed in various shootouts and bombings in the Chicago area alone. Gang violence also entered into several Chicago elections. In the Cicero mayoral elections in 1924, Capone's troops terrorized the polling places, seized opposition ballots at gunpoint, and abducted voters and election workers. The terror campaign worked: Capone's hand-picked candidate became mayor, giving the mobster practical control over the town. In a 1928 primary campaign for state attorney, the Capone mob set off bombs, murdered a supporter of the rival candidate, and engaged in election-day violence in an ultimately unsuccessful effort to lift its candidate to victory. Even in Chicago, a town with a notorious reputation for election fraud and violence, Capone's brand of intimidation and brutality was remarkable.

Gangster Al Capone at the height of his power.

The Fall of Capone

The event that brought about Capone's downfall was the Valentine's Day Massacre of 1929. Up to that point, mob warfare had been quite bloody, but the gangland execution of seven unarmed men by Capone assassins created an unprecedented sensation. The story received widespread coverage all across the country, and large rewards were put up in hopes of solving the murders. The carnage also increased calls for authorities to do something about the situation in Chicago.

Other mobsters were among the first to realize that Capone had gone too far. The leaders of the biggest crime groups in the country—Capone included—gathered in Atlantic City, New Jersey, three months after the Valentine's Day killings. At this meeting, the other bosses threatened Capone with death if he did not adopt a much lower profile. Capone agreed. After the conference broke up, he stopped in Philadelphia, where, in a prearranged set-up, he was arrested for possession of an illegal firearm and sentenced to a year in jail. By temporarily removing Capone from the scene, the gangsters hoped that mounting public concern about organized crime would subside.

A group of prominent Chicagoans, however, expressed dissatisfaction with Capone's brief incarceration. They recognized that his reign would only be terminated by death or a long prison sentence. Led by Frank Loesch, who headed the Chicago Crime Commission, this group appealed to President Herbert Hoover for help. Hoover agreed and turned the matter over to the Treasury Department.

The entrance of treasury officials into the effort to nail Capone reflected a strategic shift in the U.S. government's pursuit of prominent criminals that were defying Prohibition. Rather than pursuing them for alcohol violations or other offenses, the government was learning that it was easier to snare the criminals with charges of income tax evasion and other financial crimes.

This strategy proved especially effective in the case of Capone. Although he had engaged in bootlegging, murder, and other crimes, he had been careful to leave most of the dirty work to others, so it was difficult to prove such charges. For tax crimes, though, the government had a somewhat easier task. Investigators simply needed to prove that Capone had earned a substantial amount of money that he had failed to declare as income.

Like most mob leaders, Capone was careful to conduct most of his transactions in cash, so there were few paper records to implicate him in wrongdoing. When he emerged from his year in jail, Capone was aware that federal authorities—the so-called "Feds"—were after him, but he remained unconcerned.

Capone's confidence proved misplaced. The treasury agents built their case carefully. The primary evidence of income came from ledgers that had been seized from one of Capone's gambling houses as well as from the testimony of a former employee. In March 1931, the mobster was indicted, and later that year he was convicted of five counts of income-tax evasion. He was sentenced to eleven years in prison and required to pay $80,000 in fines and court costs. Capone's days as a crime boss were over. His criminal organization lived on, however. So did the old North Side Gang, which had survived the Valentine's Day Massacre. Both groups continued to haunt Chicago long after Prohibition came to an end.

New York: The Young Get Stronger

Chicago provides the most colorful example of how organized criminals operated during Prohibition, but mobsters were present in all the major cities. As in Chicago, they came to dominate the bootlegging industry because they were well organized, had well-developed "protection" arrangements with the authorities, and were willing to eliminate anyone who challenged them. As in Chicago, the biggest problem faced by the gangs in other cities was competition amongst themselves.

This was certainly true in New York City. Inter-gang warfare occurred there, but it was less brazen than in Chicago. There were fewer raging gun battles in the city streets, and fewer spectacular murders that were documented in the press. Another major difference was that, in New York, the gangs eventually negotiated treaties that brought relative peace to the underground. These agreements were maintained in one form or another by the city's organized crime syndicates for the rest of the twentieth century.

The body of a gangster lies on a New York sidewalk, a victim of the violent underworld struggle for control of the illicit liquor trade.

New York's mobster conflicts were a tangled web during Prohibition, but the most important struggle in the criminal underworld was between veteran "traditionalists" and a younger stable of bold, innovative mobsters. The older generation included gang leaders such as Giuseppe "Joe the Boss" Masseria and Salvatore Maranzano. These old-school veterans were bitter rivals who eventually went to all-out war with one another in 1930. This bitter blood feud, which came to be known as the Castellammarese War, degenerated into a vicious cycle of retribution that eventually claimed the lives of more than sixty people.

The younger generation of bosses, meanwhile, included men such as "Lucky" Luciano (see biography on Luciano, p. 115), Vito Genovese, and Arthur Fleganhiemer, alias "Dutch" Schultz, who controlled much of the city's illegal alcohol trade in the late 1920s and early 1930s. These men were allied with the older generation, and even took part in the battles waged by the elders. But the younger mobsters shared a different vision of the future. Like Johnny Torrio in Chicago, they favored cooperation among gangs—even among gangs from different ethnic backgrounds. For example, although Luciano was born in Italy, he was close with Jewish gangsters Ben "Bugsy" Siegel and Meyer Lansky, among others. They reasoned that if they were not distracted by battles with their fellow mobsters, they would be better equipped to establish and maintain smooth-running, efficient, highly profitable operations.

Playing Cards with Lucky

It was Lucky Luciano who broke the deadly stalemate between Masseria and Maranzano. Luciano had risen to prominence thanks to Masseria, who had made Lucky his top lieutenant in 1927. By 1931 Masseria had developed doubts about the depth of Luciano's loyalty, but officially Lucky was still on the Masseria "team."

One spring day in 1931, Luciano and his boss had lunch together at an Italian restaurant on Coney Island. After eating, the men played cards for several hours while the restaurant emptied out. At about 3:30, Lucky left the table to use the bathroom. As soon as he was gone, four men walked up behind Masseria and put five bullets into him. According to legend, he died clutching the ace of diamonds. Moments after the gunmen fled, Luciano returned from the bathroom. He pretended to be shocked. "Why would anyone want to kill poor Joe?" he asked.

For a short time Salvatore Maranzano was allowed to believe that he was "boss of bosses," but then Luciano and his collaborators struck again. In September 1931, four men killed Maranzano in his Manhattan office. According to some accounts, as many as fifty other "old-line" mafia members were killed on the same day—a purge of the elder generation all across the country. Other scholars, such as Thomas Reppetto in his book *American Mafia*, dispute this and suggest that there were only a handful of related killings.

Whatever the case, historians agree that Luciano became one of the top figures in organized crime after the death of Maranzano. Some contend that he became the new boss of bosses. Others believe that Luciano was content to manage his own operations and provide guidance to other syndicates as needed. Prior to his conviction in 1936 for running a prostitution network, Luciano helped foster an alliance among gang leaders in various parts of the country, especially in the Northeast and the Midwest. He also established a means of arbitrating differences between the mobsters, which helped avoid bloody conflicts. The alignment of the New York crime "families" that he oversaw still exists today.

From the 1930s onward, the government enjoyed some success in prosecuting prominent gangsters, including Luciano. But these convictions did not threaten the underlying organization of the mob in any serious way. By the end of Prohibition, organized crime had become a resilient and seemingly permanent part of the American landscape.

Chapter Seven
OPPOSITION AND REFORM

—⊷⊶—

"The saloon is still here, and more people are engaged in the business than in pre-Volstead days. You did not exterminate the brewery. You made millions of little breweries and installed them in the homes of the people."

—Senator James A. Reed
addressing Prohibition supporters in the Senate, 1929

Within a few years of its adoption, all of the major problems of Prohibition had made themselves known. The law was not being obeyed, it was not being enforced very effectively, it was breeding corruption, and it was enriching criminals. Nonetheless, the Eighteenth Amendment remained in effect for more than thirteen years. This was partly due to the fact that it is difficult to undo a constitutional amendment—a new amendment has to be passed to repeal the old one. But another reason why Prohibition lasted so long was that the debate over alcohol remained as politically charged as ever.

Many drys refused to admit Prohibition's shortcomings because to do so would weaken their cause and give fresh ammunition to critics who believed that the amendment should never have been passed in the first place. Instead, many Prohibition advocates maintained that the laws were working fine, despite all evidence to the contrary. This attitude made it difficult to fix the problems, but some attempts at reform were undertaken during the second half of the 1920s. The results of these efforts were mixed.

Cleaning up the Prohibition Unit

Despite the widespread corruption in the Prohibition Unit, Commissioner Roy Haynes remained at the helm of the agency from 1921 to 1927. Haynes offered a perpetually upbeat, sunny perspective on the battle to enforce Prohibition, doling out positive pronouncements such as "the amendment is being enforced to an even greater extent than many devoted friends anticipated" and "bootleg patronage has fallen off fifty percent."

These claims were seldom supported by facts. But despite the floundering performance of the Prohibition Unit in the early 1920s, the staunch support of Wayne Wheeler of the Anti-Saloon League (ASL) enabled Haynes to keep his position. Ultimately, however, Wheeler's influence had its limitations. In 1925, General Lincoln C. Andrews was appointed assistant secretary of treasury in charge of Prohibition. Haynes retained his title of commissioner, but his authority was greatly reduced as Andrews assumed many of his duties.

General Andrews was determined to reform the Prohibition Unit. One of his first priorities was to do away with the incompetent officers that had been appointed through political patronage. As he explained in a letter to the unit's personnel, agents would be "selected for merit only, and in accordance with personal fitness and qualifications," which would result in "a clean-cut business organization." It was an ambitious plan—and in the end it proved too ambitious to succeed. Politicians were quite happy with their system of awarding jobs to valuable supporters, so they resisted Andrews's efforts. The general's plan languished. So did his request for increased funding for the agency.

A year and a half after Andrews first submitted his plan, Congress finally responded to the general's call for changes in the unit's hiring practices (his requests for additional funding were ignored). In 1927 Congress passed a bill that reorganized the Prohibition Unit and required Prohibition agents to pass Civil Service exams (the agency was renamed the Prohibition Bureau at this time). The Civil Service tests revealed the poor caliber of men who had been hired under the patronage system. Nearly three out of every four agents failed the test. So many failed, in fact, that the agency had to develop an easier test, and even then it had difficulty filling positions. The new hiring guidelines helped to reduce corruption somewhat, but they failed to end bribe-taking altogether. After all, the payoff system was well established, and the agency remained underfunded and understaffed.

Alcohol and Industry

Many business leaders were initially in favor of Prohibition, believing that it would make the workforce more sober and more productive. Some of these industrialists later changed their opinion after seeing the effects of the Eighteenth Amendment. Among those who shifted sides were John D. Rockefeller Jr. and Pierre S. Du Pont. When he announced his reasons for opposing Prohibition, Rockefeller noted that "respect for all law has been greatly lessened" and he complained that "a vast army of lawbreakers has been recruited and financed on a colossal scale." But he and other corporate leaders had another reason to promote repeal. Both income and corporate taxes had increased steadily since the late 1910s. If alcohol became legal once more, the government would get a share of liquor sales, which might lessen the tax burden on individuals and businesses.

But such incentives meant nothing to Henry Ford, who never wavered from his anti-alcohol stance. In the following passage from the September 1929 issue of *Pictorial Review*, he stands by the argument that Prohibition resulted in greater workplace efficiency.

> If booze ever comes back to the United States, I am thru with manufacturing. I would not be bothered with the problem of handling over two hundred thousand men and trying to pay them wages which the saloons would take away from them. I would not be interested in putting automobiles in the hands of a generation soggy with drink.
>
> With booze in control we can count on only two or three effective days' work a week in the factories—and that would destroy the short day and the five-day week which sober industry has introduced. When men were drunk two or three days a week, industry had to have a ten- or twelve-hour day and a seven-day week. With sobriety the working man can have an eight-hour day and a five-day week with the same or greater pay.

When repeal came, however, Ford reconsidered his vow to close up his plants. In fact, he even served beer at the unveiling of one of his new car models shortly after repeal became effective—an occurrence that shocked most observers.

Shifting Political Winds

The changes at the Prohibition Bureau reflected a gradual shift in political power. The drys and the Anti-Saloon League, in particular, were losing their absolute hold on Congress. The hearings that led to the reorganization of the agency gave wet politicians the chance to publicize their opposition to Prohibition and to heap scorn on the ASL. Senator Edward I. Edwards of New Jersey called the league "un-American, entirely selfish, bigoted, and intolerant." By the late 1920s, the anti-Prohibition forces did not yet have sufficient support to consider repealing the Eighteenth Amendment, but they were becoming stronger with each passing year.

Another sign of the political shift was the growing prominence of organizations opposed to Prohibition. The most powerful was the Association against the Prohibition Amendment (AAPA). Though it had been around since 1918, the group became a formidable force in the late 1920s after it attracted powerful business leaders such as Pierre S. Du Pont. These wealthy supporters kept the group well financed, which allowed the AAPA to pursue many of the same tactics previously used by the ASL. They surveyed candidates throughout the country and threw their support behind those that supported wet policies. They also cranked out reams of anti-Prohibition literature.

An offshoot organization, the Women's Organization for National Prohibition Reform (WONPR) showed that the wets could also produce their own female activists. WONPR was led by Pauline Sabin, the wife of a prominent New York banker. She set the standard for the so-called "Sabine Women" who made up WONPR: they were largely wealthy, stylish members of high society who knew how to attract coverage from newspapers. More importantly, they weakened the drys' claim that the vast majority of women favored Prohibition.

The drys realized the threat the repeal-minded women posed, repeatedly lashing out at them in the press. A pro-Prohibition paper called the *American Independent*, for example, derided the Sabine Women as the "scum of the earth, parading around in skirts, and possibly late at night flirting with other women's husbands at drunken and fashionable resorts."

At the same time that opposition groups gained strength, the ASL began having internal problems. Wayne Wheeler died suddenly of a heart attack in 1927. The loss of this nationally known Prohibition advocate was a major blow to the cause. Bishop James Cannon, a longtime ASL executive, took over

Prohibition protestors parade down a city street.

leadership of the organization. A high-ranking official in the Methodist Episcopal Church, Cannon was known as one of the ASL's most morally upright members, denouncing gambling, racy dancing, and various other activities in addition to alcohol. But beginning in 1929, he became implicated in several scandals. He was accused of misappropriating campaign money, participating in questionable "bucket shop" investments—in effect, gambling on stocks—and of carrying on an adulterous relationship with a female acquaintance. Cannon eventually faced a criminal trial over the campaign funds and was brought before a church tribunal on moral grounds. He was acquitted in both hearings, but his reputation was badly damaged. Many of his former supporters agreed with *Christian Century*, which called Cannon a "lost leader." Wet activists seized on his behavior as evidence of their claim that dry leaders were untrustworthy hypocrites.

Presidents and Prohibition

One of the curious facts of Prohibition is that it did not become a major issue in a presidential campaign until 1928. Most would-be presidents in the 1910s tended the straddle the fence on the issue—not wishing to alienate wets or drys. In the 1920s, both Warren G. Harding and Calvin Coolidge supported Prohibition, but their position was not a major issue in their elections. In 1928, however, the growing opposition to Prohibition made it a point of contention between the two candidates. Republican Herbert Hoover wanted to stay the course. In his speech accepting the party's nomination, he declared that "I do not favor the repeal of the Eighteenth Amendment," and he called for "efficient enforcement of the laws." While Hoover did concede that "grave abuses have occurred—abuses which must be remedied," he stood by the general concept of banning alcohol. In one famous passage, he described Prohibition as "a great social and economic experiment, noble in motive and far-reaching in purpose."

> *Hoover described Prohibition as "a great social and economic experiment, noble in motive and far-reaching in purpose."*

His challenger, Democrat Al Smith, took a harder line against the Eighteenth Amendment (see biography on Smith, p. 130). In his nomination acceptance speech at the Democratic convention, he described the state of Prohibition as "entirely unsatisfactory to the great many of our people." He vowed that as president he would "allow each state to determine for itself what it wants to do about the question of local habits." In essence, this meant the repeal of the Eighteenth Amendment and a return to pre-1919 conditions, when states could enact their own alcohol legislation.

Smith's opposition to Prohibition extended beyond his presidential platform. He was the governor of New York State, a wet stronghold, and he was a native of New York City, which, in the mind of ardent Prohibitionists, was the most evil town of all—"Satan's seat," in the words of Bishop Cannon. Also, Smith owed his early political successes to the backing of the Tammany Hall political machine. Tammany had a well-earned reputation for corruption, and in pre-Prohibition times it had relied on saloons as a means of organizing support. In addition, Smith was a Catholic who had earned a reputation for defending the interests of immigrants, many of whom shared his faith. Smith's candidacy thus managed to touch on many of the issues that had brought about Prohibition in the first place.

Smith's position on alcohol became the basis of negative attacks. Hoover supporters suggested that because Smith opposed Prohibition, he had a drinking problem. They frequently cited a sensational article in *The Nation* in which writer Oswald Garrison Willard stated that he had been "reliably informed" that Smith "drinks every day, and the number of his cocktails and highballs is variously estimated at from four to eight." In addition, Bishop James Cannon of the ASL (having not yet fallen from grace) made vicious attacks on Smith's support of immigrants. In a campaign speech in Cambridge, Massachusetts, Cannon revived some of the hateful rhetoric that had been used to promote Prohibition at the turn of the century:

President Herbert Hoover supported Prohibition for most of his time in the Oval Office.

> Governor Smith wants the Italians, the Sicilians, the Poles, and the Russian Jews. That kind has given us a stomach ache. We have been unable to assimilate such people in our national life, so we shut the door to them. But Smith says "give me that kind of people." He wants the kind of dirty people that you find today on the sidewalks of New York.

Mabel Walker Willebrandt, who campaigned for fellow Republican Hoover, also joined in the attacks on Smith. She urged a group of Methodist Episcopal ministers to join forces against the New York governor, which led to charges that she was making Smith's Catholicism an issue. Willebrandt denied this, but others were quite willing to hold Smith's religious beliefs against him. The anti-Catholic and pro-Prohibition Ku Klux Klan, for example, staged cross burnings along Smith's campaign route.

When the election was held in November, Hoover won by a wide margin. Prohibition alone did not account for the outcome. The economy—always a primary factor in presidential elections—was still booming in 1928, and Hoover was viewed as the best bet for maintaining the status quo because he belonged to the same party as the previous president, Calvin Coolidge. The most striking aspect of the election was that the Republican Hoover managed to carry eight traditionally Democratic southern states.

George Wickersham, head of the Wickersham Commission, at his office in Washington, D.C.

Historians attribute these results to the South's largely Protestant character and the widespread support for Prohibition in the region's rural communities.

Prohibition under the Microscope

During the campaign, Hoover had promised that, if elected, he would appoint a commission to examine the issues surrounding Prohibition. After taking office in early 1929, he formed the National Commission on Law Observance and Enforcement, which became better known as the Wickersham Commission, after its chairman, George W. Wickersham. The commission's eleven members conducted a thorough analysis that extended over two years and cost $500,000. The information they collected was later published in five large volumes, and much of it was critical of Prohibition. The statements and transcripts detailed the problems of enforcement and corruption, and portions of the report suggested that the amendment was breeding a general disregard for law and order throughout the country. The commission also heard from supporters of the Eighteenth Amendment, but there was a large body of evidence that suggested that changes were needed.

The most important document produced by the commission was its final report, issued in January 1931, which summarized the group's findings. Each of the eleven members offered a personal statement. Of these, two supported repeal of the Eighteenth Amendment, seven recommended some type of revision, and two supported the current situation with small changes. Thus, a majority of the commissioners believed that some type of major change was needed. Nonetheless, the final "Conclusions and Recommendations" section of the report suggested only very minor alterations in enforcement. These included a call for more funding and some changes regarding the regulation of industrial and prescription alcohol.

The final report pleased no one. The press criticized the fact that a lot of time and money had been spent to reach rather obvious conclusions. Some observers suggested that the report had initially called for major and immediate revisions of the Eighteenth Amendment, but that it had been changed at the last minute at the urging of powerful Prohibition advocates. (There was evidence to back this claim: One of the commissioners made reference to such a conclusion in his personal statement.) Dry activists, meanwhile, complained that the report was too critical of Prohibition and that the actions recommended by the commission were unnecessary.

And so the government's most serious inquiry into Prohibition ended in a flurry of partisan bickering, with no clear consensus on what to do about the Eighteenth Amendment. Had other historical events not intervened, it is possible the Prohibition era could have lingered on well into the 1930s. But in the two years that elapsed between the formation of the Wickersham Commission and the issuance of its final report, America had undergone a convulsive and dramatic change. That change would soon bring the "great social and economic experiment" of Prohibition to an end.

Chapter Eight

AMENDING THE AMENDMENT

"This convention wants repeal. Your candidate wants repeal. And I am confident that the United States of America wants repeal.... I say to you now that from this date on, the Eighteenth Amendment is doomed."

—Franklin D. Roosevelt accepting the Democratic nomination for the presidency, 1932

The stock market crash of October 1929 and the Great Depression that followed cast Prohibition in a whole new light. Judged against the nation's other problems, the question of legal alcohol consumption suddenly struck many Americans as an unimportant, even frivolous issue. By November 1931, ten million people were unemployed in the United States, and the number continued to grow. Those with nothing to fall back on lost their homes and were forced to live in vast squatter camps that sprang up all across the country.

Shifting their tactics to fit the times, the wets began to argue that ending Prohibition would be a help to the economy. They pointed out that taxes on legal alcohol sales would boost the cash-strapped treasury and could help finance government-assistance and job-creation programs. In addition, more money would be freed up because the Prohibition Bureau and other enforcement efforts would no longer be necessary. Those in favor of repeal also maintained that legalizing alcohol would create new jobs at breweries, distilleries, wholesale companies, liquor stores, and bars. (This argument ignored the fact that many people were already employed in the illegal versions of these businesses, so the net gain in jobs after repeal might have been quite modest.)

A woman proclaims her support for repeal of the Eighteenth Amendment.

In addition to the economic and political factors, there was also an ideological shift that made many people believe that the Eighteenth Amendment was no longer relevant. In subtle ways, Prohibition had become associated with the causes of the Depression. The corruption of police and politicians was seen as similar to the unsound financial activity that had brought economic ruin to so many. Also, there was a sense that old, impractical ideas needed to be swept aside so that the nation could make a new start. Prohibition was at the top of that list.

For all of these reasons, the hard times of the 1930s proved decisive in ending Prohibition. But Prohibition nonetheless lingered for many months. The constitutional logistics of ending the grand social experiment presented a major challenge. The only way to fully end Prohibition was to adopt another amendment repealing the Eighteenth Amendment. This required passage by a two-thirds majority in both houses of Congress and then ratification by three-quarters of the states. Even with the changed mood in the country, wets knew they would have a difficult time finding enough votes in the House and Senate. Dry senator Morris Sheppard ridiculed their chances of success as well. "There is as much chance of repealing the Eighteenth Amendment," he told the Associated Press in 1930, "as there is for a humming-bird to fly to the planet Mars with the Washington Monument tied to its tail."

Getting around the Constitution

Since so many people believed that repeal was impossible, various other solutions were discussed. One was nullification, which essentially meant that the Eighteenth Amendment would be ignored in places where the majority of the population was opposed to it. In a sense, nullification was already taking place because authorities were unable, and in some cases unwilling, to enforce the law. Some argued that a more formal means of nullification might take place if local laws were passed allowing alcohol to be sold. If these statutes were challenged in court, some believed the Supreme Court would bow to public sentiment and allow the laws to stand.

Legislators also pondered an overhaul of the Volstead Act—the laws that enforced the Eighteenth Amendment. For instance, the definition of what constituted an illegal beverage could be changed. The Volstead Act had set the level at 0.5 percent alcohol, but it could be raised to 3 or 4 percent, which would allow "real" beer to be sold and manufactured legally. Another alternative would be to revise the law so that each state could determine for itself what percentage of alcohol was permissible. This approach ran the same risk as nullification: the revised law could be interpreted as unconstitutional. Again, the matter would have to be decided by the Supreme Court.

In the end, none of these methods was attempted. The country limped through two years of the Depression with Prohibition still in place. As 1932 dawned, the country began to prepare for the presidential election that would be held in November of that year. The contest promised to be a referendum on President Hoover's handling of the economy, but alcohol became another issue differentiating the candidates.

Hoover vs. Roosevelt

When he had run against Al Smith in 1928, Hoover's support for Prohibition had not hurt his campaign. Times had changed, however. At the 1932 Republican convention, some members urged the party to oppose Prohibition. Others remained firm supporters. This clash of opinions was reflected in the party's platform. It called for a resubmission of the Eighteenth Amendment to the states (having them re-vote on the same measure) but did not support outright repeal. This made the Republicans and President Hoover partly wet and partly dry—or "moist," to borrow the term of historian Sean Dennis Cashman.

The Democratic nominee was Franklin D. Roosevelt. As a state senator in New York Roosevelt had voted dry on occasion but had generally promoted the idea of letting local communities decide their own policies on alcohol. After being elected governor of New York in 1928, he had followed a similar course. By 1932 he could see which way the wind was blowing, and so he joined with the rest of his party in calling for repeal of the Eighteenth Amendment.

A Saloon by Any Other Name

The negative aspects of the saloon had driven alcohol reform since the 1800s, and its shady reputation was not ignored in the fight for repeal of the Eighteenth Amendment. Most of those who wanted Prohibition overturned insisted that they were still opposed to the saloon. In his inauguration address, Franklin Roosevelt told the Democrats that "we must rightly and morally prevent the return of the saloon." He reiterated that message when he announced that the Twenty-first Amendment had been ratified: "I ask especially that no state by law or otherwise authorize the return of the saloon either in its old form or in some modern guise."

The "modern guise" is exactly what came to be, however. Legal drinking establishments opened everywhere as "bars," "lounges," and—reviving the old colonial term—"taverns." Politicians took few steps to reform the trade, aside from some rather ridiculous ones. New York, for instance, made it illegal for a drinking establishment to call itself a saloon. On the positive side, the worst characteristics of the old saloons became less prevalent following Prohibition. The barroom-based political machines no longer had their old clout, and the alcohol industry avoided the worst of its previous abuses. Today, there are still bars that harbor prostitutes and criminals, but on the whole, modern drinking establishments have a far better reputation than those of the pre-Prohibition era.

Hoover was watching the political winds as well. In August—two months after the Republican convention—he suddenly announced that he, too, was against Prohibition. In doing this, Hoover turned his back on his party's platform and on his previous position on alcohol. The Prohibition experiment was apparently not as noble as he had once proclaimed. Now he felt that the Eighteenth Amendment caused "disrespect not only of this law but all laws," as well as "a degeneration in municipal government and an increase in subsidized crime and violence." The sudden change of heart may have hurt Hoover more than it helped him, as it made him appear insincere and opportunistic. At any rate, the conversion failed to negate other criticisms of his record, including charges that his administration's fiscal policies had helped bring about and prolong the Depression.

When the vote took place in November, Roosevelt won election in a landslide. In addition, Democrats—many of them wet—dominated the congressional races, giving the party solid majorities in both the House and Senate. Suddenly, repeal had gone from impossible to quite likely. If Prohibition had been tied to the Depression in the public's mind, repeal now became linked to the optimism surrounding Roosevelt's New Deal program. In fact, ending Prohibition became the new administration's first priority.

The Twenty-First Amendment

A resolution calling for repeal of the Eighteenth Amendment was introduced in December 1932, just a month after the election. The following February, after the newly elected Congress was seated, the resolution passed both the House and Senate with the necessary two-thirds majorities. The new amendment then went to the states for ratification. The wording of the Twenty-first Amendment specifically required the states to vote on ratification "by convention" rather than by a vote of their legislators. This meant that the states had to hold special elections to choose delegates to the convention. In April, Michigan became the first state to ratify the Twenty-First Amendment, but gaining the necessary three-fourths majority was expected to take another year or longer.

In the meantime, Roosevelt started dismantling Prohibition in other ways. He slashed the Prohibition Bureau's funding by more than half. More importantly—at least to those clamoring for legal brew—he called on Congress to modify the Volstead Act so that beer containing 3.2 percent alcohol could be manufactured and sold. Congress complied, and on April 7, 1933, legally brewed beer with significant alcohol content flowed once more. In St. Louis, 30,000 people descended on the Anheuser-Busch brewery, where a convoy of beer trucks stretched for twenty blocks to serve the thirsty. Similar scenes of revelry took place all across the country. On the first day, 1.5 million barrels were consumed nationwide. On the second day, many places went dry once again—simply because the supplies had been exhausted.

Just like the Eighteenth Amendment, the Twenty-First Amendment sped through the ratification process far more quickly than anticipated. In just eight months, thirty-five states approved the amendment. On December 5, 1933, Utah became number thirty-six, and the amendment became part of the United States Constitution. It was once again legal to sell, manufacture,

A crowd gathers as kegs of beer are unloaded in front of a restaurant in New York City on the morning of April 7, 1933, when low-alcohol beer was legalized once again.

and transport alcoholic beverages in the United States (assuming there was no state law to the contrary).

Due to various bureaucratic delays involving licenses and supplies, the celebration of the passage of the Twenty-First Amendment was more subdued than the one that had greeted the arrival of 3.2 beer. Several cities staged ceremonies where effigies of Prohibition were killed. They harkened back to the Rev. Billy Sunday's funeral for John Barleycorn in 1920, gloating that the reverend's claim that "King Alcohol" was dead had been proven wrong. Prohibition, on the other hand, had expired after thirteen years, ten months, and eighteen days. But its influence would last much longer.

Chapter Nine

THE LEGACY
OF PROHIBITION

"In its simplistic determination to strike at the root of 'social evil' without any thought of the consequences, or of the means required to enforce it, Prohibition was a striking example of the American propensity to believe that society was infinitely malleable and that all it would take to rid America of its blemishes and turn it into a promised land would be a few well-meaning laws."

—Edward Behr, *Prohibition:*
Thirteen Years That Changed America

When Prohibition was over, no one really wanted to talk about it. Memoirs of the prominent figures of the era give surprisingly little space to the subject, though it was one of the most important issues in American politics over the span of two decades. With time, however, Prohibition's enduring lessons have become clear.

The first is that passing laws to regulate personal conduct is no simple task—at least not in a country as diverse as the United States. Prohibition proved conclusively that it takes more than legislation to bring about a fundamental change in the way Americans live. The banning of alcohol and the resistance to that ban was actually the continuation of an ongoing debate about how laws should function in the United States. On one side were those who believed that statutes regulating personal conduct were good and necessary. Andrew Volstead, sponsor of the Volstead Act, succinctly summed up the feelings of many Prohibitionists when he said that "law regulates morality, law has regulated morality since the ten commandments." The opposing view was that American perspectives on the morality of alcohol consumption ranged quite widely, and that laws that treaded into this area were onerous and should be resisted. "No man was ever made good by force," wrote Bolton Hall in his book *Thrift*.

The events of Prohibition showed that the second argument ultimately won the day. As Andrew Sinclair observed in *Prohibition: Era of Excess*, the Prohibitionists seriously misjudged their support. They believed that public opinion was firmly behind them and that "the work of enforcement officials would be a mere matter of arresting the guilty few with the approval of the righteous many." This misjudgment is the primary reason why so little fore-thought was given to the issue of Prohibition enforcement.

Prohibition as a Breeder of Cynicism

Scholars also believe that the Prohibition era bred increased and wide-spread cynicism about the integrity of the American political system and about the country's laws in general. This outcome was foreseen by New York Congressman Fiorello La Guardia even before Prohibition took effect. "If this law fails to be enforced—as it most certainly will be as it is drawn—it will create contempt and disregard for the law all over the country," he warned Congressman Volstead in 1919.

This decline in faith in American public institutions was exacerbated by the thousands of government officials who accepted payoffs to preserve alcohol traffic or to protect lawbreakers from prosecution. Corruption was not an invention of the 1920s: in fact, shady saloon politics had helped bring about the Eighteenth Amendment. But during Prohibition, payoffs were more wide-spread and were conducted more openly than ever before. This gave the public the sense that the entire political system was unjust, and it seemed to give official sanction to greedy, unscrupulous behavior in other realms of American society. At the beginning of the twenty-first century, it is fair to say that American cynicism about their elected representatives and other societal institutions was on the rise. That skepticism—which persists today—was not created by Prohibition alone. But the events of the 1920s and early 1930s certainly made it more widespread and helped set the tone for the modern era.

The sense of distrust was enhanced by the fact that Prohibition had a far more deleterious impact on the poor than the rich. Activist Pauline Sabin has

Chicago bartenders pour a round of drinks for celebrants upon hearing that the Eighteenth Amendment has been repealed.

even called it "the greatest piece of class legislation ever enacted in this country." By the time Prohibition became the law of the land, the chasm between America's affluent and impoverished classes was already significant, and the Eighteenth Amendment seemed to further widen—or at least highlight—this gap. While the more affluent could afford to frequent romantic and stylish nightspots, the increased price of bootleg alcohol left poor working Americans with alcoholic drinks that were often foul at best and poisonous at worst. The era's widespread corruption also deepened the class divisions. While it became common for the wealthy and well-connected to buy their way out of alcohol charges, poor Americans were far more likely to receive stiff fines or jail sentences for transgressions of Prohibition law.

Prohibition's Boost to Organized Crime

Organized crime had been around long before Prohibition and it would continue long after the Eighteenth Amendment was repealed. But Prohibition did prove instrumental in its growth and modernization. Alcohol profits provided gangsters with large infusions of money, which in turn helped them to expand their illegal activities. The struggle over bootlegging dollars created bloody discord among the different gangs, but by the end of Prohibition they had found ways to mediate their disagreements and emerged as stronger and better-coordinated organizations.

Prohibition also bestowed a veneer of glamour and legitimacy on mobsters in the alcohol trade. Some people who disapproved of the ban on alcohol looked kindly on the criminals who helped provide the bootleg booze. Also, the mobsters' bootlegging riches marked them as successful, and that success was admired and envied. Even those who disapproved of the gangsters followed their exploits with a certain fascination.

Those who romanticized the booze-running gangsters probably changed their mind when Prohibition ended. At that point, the mob's less attractive side became more visible. The organized crime syndicates sponsored illegal gambling and prostitution. They threatened legitimate business owners, forcing them to pay "protection" money, which in turn drove up the costs of goods and services for consumers. They continued to corrupt public officials and interfere with the democratic process. The wealth the mobsters acquired from their alcohol operations also allowed them to move into new areas, such as controlling labor unions. Finally, the networks they had developed for smuggling and distributing alcohol were easily converted to another product—illegal drugs. Organized crime had dealt in substances such as cocaine and heroin before Prohibition, but they expanded these operations afterward. These drugs continue to be an important source of mob money today.

Prohibition and Women

Not all of Prohibition's influences were negative. The debate over alcohol proved an important motivation for women to enter the political arena, and it illustrated the power they could bring to bear. The Women's War of the 1870s showed that female activists could be extremely effective at stirring public sentiment, and the prolonged support of the National Women's Christian Temperance Union was instrumental in the eventual passage of the Eighteenth Amendment.

It is often assumed that Prohibition was partly attributable to women gaining the right to vote, but many historians believe that their role in passing the Eighteenth Amendment was limited. Nationwide suffrage came in 1920—after Prohibition had been enacted. Prior to that point, women could vote only in certain states and in some local areas. And in some locales their participation was limited to certain types of elections (such as those dealing with education and taxes). Women were active members of the electorate in the 1920s and 1930s, however, which gave them a direct say in the course of political events. Perhaps the most striking aspect of female involvement in Prohibition was women's diversity of perspectives on the issue.

"No man was ever made good by force," wrote Bolton Hall.

Initially, it was widely assumed that women were overwhelmingly opposed to alcohol, but that belief changed with the formation of the Women's Organization for National Prohibition Reform (WONPR). The activities of WONPR proved that women could stake out opinions all across the political spectrum and that they were not a one-dimensional political bloc that could be taken for granted. Also, the era saw the emergence of several prominent female political leaders, including WONPR's Pauline Sabin and assistant attorney general Mabel Walker Willebrandt.

Prohibition also ushered in a new female archetype in American society. The appearance of the liberated "flapper" of the 1920s heralded new heights of social and sexual freedom for women. The presence of females in the barrooms was one of the most dramatic symbols of that freedom.

Prohibition and the Rise of Lobbying

In the aftermath of Prohibition, the Anti-Saloon League was widely condemned for its imperious behavior and inability to compromise. Despite these shortcomings, however, the ASL became the model for issue-oriented lobbying groups seeking political power. In *The Great Illusion*, Herbert Asbury maintained that the ASL ran "the most efficient propaganda machine in American history." After masterminding the passage of the Eighteenth Amendment, the league called itself "the strongest political organization in the world." It was an exaggeration but not an outrageous one. The ASL's influence could already be seen during the Prohibition era, when opposing groups such as the Association against the Prohibition Amendment copied their tactics. In the decades since, ASL-style lobbying efforts have been emulated by organizations across the political spectrum to press their views on abortion, the environment, the Second Amendment, and other issues.

On the other hand, Prohibition also illustrated the potentially disproportionate impact of groups such as the ASL on policymaking in America. "The lessons of Prohibition are plain," wrote Andrew Sinclair in *Prohibition: The Era of Excess*. "The fine frenzy of a minority, a long period of indoctrination, a powerful pressure group, and a state of national fear can cause the adoption of an ill-considered reform."

Prohibition and the Constitution

Finally, the Prohibition experiment has been cited as a factor in the United States' reluctance to amend the Constitution since the 1930s. Of the six amendments that have been passed since the Twenty-First Amendment repealed alcohol, most have been concerned with improving operational aspects of government rather than addressing perceived shortcomings in societal values and mores. The lone explicit exception to this rule is the Twenty-Fourth Amendment, ratified in 1964 at the height of the American civil rights movement. This amendment outlawed the use of poll taxes and other taxes that had been commonly used in cities and towns across the South to suppress the black vote.

Scholars believe that Prohibition's failure confirmed the belief in American communities that the Constitution should not be tampered with lightly, especially for the purpose of restricting personal freedoms. Today, the basic soundness of the Constitution—and the wisdom of the Founding Fathers who created it—is an accepted article of faith in American society. As a result, few of the numerous proposed amendments to the Constitution that have been introduced in Congress over the last half-century have even come close to Congressional passage, let alone state ratification.

BIOGRAPHIES

James Cannon Jr. (1864-1944)
*Bishop of the Methodist Episcopal Church, South
and Leader of the Prohibition movement*

James Cannon Jr. was born November 13, 1864, in Salisbury, Maryland, the youngest of five children. His father was James Cannon Sr., a prosperous merchant. His mother was Lydia (Primrose) Cannon, who formed a local chapter of the Women's Christian Temperance Union while Cannon was growing up. After completing high school, Cannon enrolled at Randolph-Macon College, a Methodist school in Ashland, Virginia. Even in his college years, Cannon was known for his dour personality and his insistence on lecturing fellow students about their moral shortcomings. Some of his sternest warnings were aimed at classmates that frequented saloons. Cannon later described them as "foolishly drunk, noisily drunk, stupidly drunk, disgustingly drunk, crazily drunk."

After receiving a bachelor of arts degree in 1884, Cannon relocated to New Jersey and pursued dual degrees simultaneously: a bachelor of divinity from Princeton Theological Seminary and master of arts from Princeton College. He received both in 1888 and later that same year he married Lura Virginia Bennett. Cannon then became a pastor with the Methodist Episcopal Church, South (also known as the Southern Methodist Church), holding several short-term assignments in different parts of Virginia.

An Industrious Crusader for Temperance

In 1894 Cannon became the director of the Blackstone Female Institute in Nottoway County, Virginia. At the time, it was a school in name only, having no teachers and very few facilities. Cannon later said that he "averaged nineteen hours per day of hard work" in building Blackstone into a viable school. Cannon also had his hand in a variety of publishing concerns. In 1894 he became the editor of the *Methodist Recorder*, in 1904 he took control of the *Richmond Christian Advocate*, and in 1910 he helped form the *Richmond Virginian*, a daily paper that promoted the dry agenda.

Cannon had always supported temperance, and he became deeply involved in the issue in 1901, when he helped form the Anti-Saloon League of Virginia. A year later he joined the executive committee of the national organization. Cannon played a key role in the passage of local-option laws throughout Virginia. After becoming the superintendent of the state chapter in 1909, he oversaw the passage of statewide Prohibition in 1914. In the late 1910s, he began working with another temperance organization, the World League against Alcoholism, which sought to restrict alcohol consumption in foreign countries.

Cannon's Prohibition work helped make him a rising star within the Southern Methodist organization. In 1918 he was elected as one of the church's six bishops, which gave him greater responsibilities. To manage his many affairs, Cannon put in long hours. His schedule left him little time for relaxing with his wife and children (he had nine in total, seven of which survived to adulthood). Cannon's biographer, Virginius Dabney, noted in *Dry Messiah* (1949) that "work alone—bone-crushing work—was this furious crusader's preferred form of recreation."

During this period, Cannon denounced myriad aspects of American society, from Coca-Cola to actress Sarah Bernhardt (for her "unsavory moral ideas") to dancing ("a temptation to the flesh"). One acquaintance described Cannon as "cold as a snake." Another conceded that the bishop "may not be the best beloved, but he is the most feared man in Virginia."

Promoting Prohibition

As the Anti-Saloon League (ASL) began its push for national Prohibition, Cannon became chairman of the league's legislative committee. He helped draft the Eighteenth Amendment, and he lobbied Congress and state politicians to approve it. In these activities he frequently worked alongside the ASL's Wayne Wheeler, but the two men were not friendly allies. Both were headstrong leaders and they frequently bickered with one another. By the early 1920s, Wheeler had emerged as the more powerful figure, but Cannon maintained a central role in league affairs.

With Wheeler's death in 1927, Cannon became the effective leader of the ASL. He reached the peak of his power the next year, when he waded into the 1928 presidential campaign. Like many others from the South, Cannon had been a lifelong Democrat, but he was unwilling to support the candidacy of Al Smith. Publicly, Cannon opposed Smith because the New York governor was wet, but Smith's Roman Catholic religion was also a concern.

Cannon's leadership of the so-called Anti-Smith Democrats helped bring about Smith's defeat in many southern states and showed that the drys were still a political force to be reckoned with. Shortly after the election, journalist H. L. Mencken described Cannon as "the most powerful ecclesiastic ever heard of in America." The bishop was certainly pleased with the outcome of the voting, but his happiness was muted by the ongoing illness of his wife and her death in late November 1928.

An Embattled Bishop

Cannon's power proved fleeting. In June 1929, stories broke that he had been a large customer of a New York "bucket shop" investment firm. While not illegal, such "margin" investments were speculative in nature—a form of gambling. Previously, Cannon had joined with other Methodists in denouncing "all forms of gambling," so the revelation of his investments put him in a very awkward position. Cannon's defense was that he had been unaware that the investment firm was involved in speculative trading. This excuse was shown to be a lie when some of Cannon's correspondence was later released.

More scandals soon came to light. The press reported that Cannon had been suspected of illegal profiteering during World War I because of questionable flour purchases he had made for the Blackstone Institute. He had been cleared of criminal wrongdoing in this matter, but the revelation of his wartime activity proved another embarrassment. The bishop's more recent activities also came under investigation. He was accused of misappropriating more than $71,000 in campaign funds from the 1928 elections.

In the summer of 1930, the Cannon saga took another turn. It was suddenly announced that he and a woman named Helen McCallum had gotten married in London. Shortly thereafter, newspaper stories revealed that Cannon had known McCallum before his previous wife died, that he had paid her a monthly allowance, and that he had frequently visited her at her New York apartment. Though the term was not used in the newspaper articles, Cannon was being accused of adultery.

Various charges resulted from these scandals. In 1930, Cannon was brought before a Methodist Episcopal tribunal, accused of adultery, immorality, gambling, and "gross moral turpitude." After hearing the evidence, the panel ruled in Cannon's favor, deciding that no trial was necessary. In 1931 he and his secretary Ada L. Burroughs were indicted for their handling of the campaign money. In 1934 they were acquitted, largely because a charge of conspiracy between Cannon and Burroughs was never proven.

The Lost Leader

Cannon had fared well in his legal proceedings, but not in the court of public opinion. The allegations of misconduct seriously damaged his authority and weakened support for Prohibition. One wet activist called Cannon "God's gift to the repeal cause." When he spoke at the Democratic convention in 1932, he was loudly jeered. Due to Cannon's diminished stature, Southern Methodist officials bypassed him for the position of presiding bishop. There was also a move to force Cannon out of his bishop's seat in 1934, but he had enough clout in the church to avoid this insult. He stepped down in 1938 after twenty years of service, as was the custom.

Cannon never gave up his fight against alcohol. For years after the Eighteenth Amendment was repealed, he kept maintaining that "the nation … will return to national prohibition." In the last years of his life, he lived in Richmond, Virginia, and continued to lobby for various dry initiatives, though he had little success. In September 1944, he traveled to Chicago to attend an Anti-Saloon League meeting. There, he suffered a heart attack and then a cerebral hemorrhage, which ended his life on September 6.

Sources
Coffey, Thomas M. *The Long Thirst: Prohibition in America, 1920-1933*. New York: Norton, 1975.
Dabney, Virginius. *Dry Messiah: The Life of Bishop Cannon*. New York: Alfred A. Knopf, 1949.
Hohner, Robert A. *Prohibition and Politics: The Life of Bishop James Cannon, Jr.* Columbia: University of South Carolina Press, 1999.

Al Capone (1899-1947)
Prohibition-Era Mobster

Alphonse Capone was born January 17, 1899, in Brooklyn, New York. He was the fourth of nine children born to Gabriele Capone (originally Caponi), a barber, and Teresina (Raiola) Capone, a seamstress. Capone's parents had arrived in Brooklyn in 1893 from Naples, Italy, and settled in the low-income Italian district near the Brooklyn Navy Yard. The neighborhood was also home to mobster Johnny Torrio, a cousin of Capone's who was seventeen years his elder. Torrio took a shine to the youngster and allowed him to run errands on occasion. This provided Capone's entrance into the world of organized crime. "[Torrio] made it possible for me to get my start," Capone later said.

Capone dropped out of school at age fourteen and fell in with the Five Points Gang. Even as a teenager, Capone was big and intimidating. This landed him a job as a bouncer at the Harvard Inn, which was run by underworld figure Frankie Yale. There, Capone acquired his "Scarface" nickname when he suffered two razor wounds that he carried for the rest of his life. When he was nineteen, Capone met an Irish-American woman named Mary "Mae" Coughlin. They were soon married and had a son, Albert Francis Capone, better known as Sonny. The child's godfather was Johnny Torrio, who had relocated to Chicago but remained friendly with Capone. "I looked on Johnny like my advisor and father," Capone recalled. In 1919 or 1920 Torrio offered Capone a job in his growing Chicago operation. Fearful of a possible murder charge in New York—he had badly injured a man in a barroom brawl—Capone seized the opportunity and moved his family to the Windy City.

A Rising Force in the Windy City Underworld

Capone arrived in Chicago just in time for Prohibition—and just in time to assist Torrio in his takeover of "Big Jim" Colosimo's vice operation. After performing low-level chores for a time, Capone became manager of the Four Deuces, one of Torrio's gambling and prostitution houses. Capone soon became the syndicate's second in command, and when Torrio took an extended vacation in 1923, Capone assumed temporary command of his empire. His biggest triumph during this period was his violent and ruthless campaign to swing the 1924 mayoral election in the Chicago suburb of Cicero in favor of a candidate controlled by Torrio and Capone. The election results gave the gang a vital base of operations outside the Chicago city limits.

When Torrio was wounded early the following year by a rival mob, Capone took over management of the gang's affairs. Then, in March 1925, Torrio handed Capone the keys to the whole operation. In the gang wars that followed, Capone formed alliances with other mobsters when necessary and broke them when advantageous. He ordered well-planned assassinations to eliminate rivals, usually carefully targeting specific individuals. When he strayed into large-scale killings, trouble usually followed—the Valentine's Day Massacre being the best example.

While his reputation for brutality was well earned, Capone was also a skilled organizer and strategist. He, like Johnny Torrio and Lucky Luciano, dreamed of establishing a truly national crime organization. That desire was part of the reason that he tried to maintain control of the Chicago branch of the Unione Siciliane, a cultural association linked to organized crime operations throughout the United States. Though Capone was not Sicilian, he realized the importance the organization could play in a national network of mobsters. Struggles over the group's leadership helped fuel the Chicago wars of the late 1920s.

Though he was powerful and wealthy, Capone's notoriety also stemmed from his well-developed sense of public relations. After the stock market crash of 1929, for example, he quickly opened soup kitchens for poor people, and he ordered Chicago-area merchants to give clothing and food to the needy at his expense. And when an innocent bystander was wounded in an attempt on Capone's life, the mobster made a big show of paying her hospital bill, which totaled $10,000. Rather than avoiding reporters, Capone welcomed their attention. He relentlessly sought to portray himself as a good-hearted businessman out to help others. "I'm not as black as I'm painted," he said. "I've got a heart in me.... I can't stand to see anybody hungry or cold or helpless. Many a poor family in Chicago thinks I'm Santa Claus."

In 1928 Capone purchased a mansion on Palm Island, near Miami, Florida. He began to split his time between Chicago and south Florida, a place he described as "the sunny Italy of the New World." There, he frequently entertained sports figures and show-business personalities such as Al Jolson and Eddie Cantor, which added to his fame.

Even after he was indicted for tax evasion and bootlegging, Capone skillfully played the press, presenting himself as a harmless businessman that had been made a scapegoat. While he admitted that he had been involved in providing alcohol, he denied that he was part of a criminal organization. "Honestly," he told reporters, "there is not, nor has there ever been what might be called a Capone gang." Instead, he portrayed himself as an agent of good. "I have always been opposed to violence—to shootings," he told them. "I have fought, yes, but fought for peace."

Behind Bars

Following his conviction, Capone was sent to the Atlanta Penitentiary in May 1933, where he worked as a shoe cobbler. But his money and stature ensured special privileges even inside the prison. He had his own crew of inmate bodyguards and was able to commandeer the prisoner's tennis court whenever he wished. These favors ended when he was transferred to Alcatraz, a new maximum-security prison on an island in San Francisco Bay. At Alcatraz he worked in the prison laundry and endured the same prison conditions as the rest of the prisoners.

In 1938 Capone began experiencing temporary spells of dementia. Tests by prison doctors revealed that he was suffering from paresis of the brain—a result of having contracted syphilis at some earlier point in his life. The treatments he undertook at Alcatraz slowed the disease but could not cure it. After transfer to a prison near Los Angeles, Capone gained his freedom in November 1939 (his sentence had been reduced for good behavior). Many people expected Capone to return to his life of crime, but when Jake Guzik, one of the members of the Capone gang, was questioned about the possibility, he dismissed the idea. "Al," he said, "is nutty as a fruitcake."

Capone returned to his home on Palm Island, where he remained for the rest of his life. He alternated between periods of lucid thought and derangement. Perhaps because of his approval of numerous drive-by shootings during his Chicago years, he developed an extreme fear of automobiles, the mere sight of which caused him to panic. In January 1947 he suffered a brain hemorrhage. After hanging on for nearly a week, he died on January 25.

Capone's death was mourned by some and celebrated by many others. The *New York Times* captured the prevailing reaction to his passing when it described him in an editorial as "the symbol of a shameful era, the monstrous symptom of a disease which was eating into the conscience of America. Looking back on it now, this period of Prohibition in full, ugly flower seems fantastically incredible. Capone himself was incredible, the creation of an evil dream."

Sources

Bergreen, Laurence. *Capone: The Man and the Era*. New York: Simon and Schuster, 1994.
Iorizzo, Luciano. *Al Capone: A Biography*. Westport, CT: Greenwood Press, 2003.
Kobler, John. *Capone: The Life and World of Al Capone*. New York: G. P. Putnam's Sons, 1971.
Schoenberg, Robert. *Mr. Capone*. New York: Morrow, 1992.

Warren G. Harding (1865-1923)
President of the United States during First Years of Prohibition

Warren Gamaliel Harding was born November 2, 1865, near Blooming Grove, Ohio. He was the oldest of eight children born to George Tryon Harding and Phoebe (Dickerson) Harding. Warren's parents were farmers at the time of his birth, but his father later became a doctor and moved the family to Marion, Ohio. Harding attended Ohio Central College in the town of Iberia. After graduation, he became interested in newspaper work, and in 1884 he purchased a struggling paper, the Marion *Star*, eventually turning it into a profitable business. In 1891 Harding married Florence Kling De Wolfe, a widow with one child.

The *Star* supported the Republican Party, and in time Harding became heavily involved in Ohio politics. In 1898 he was elected to the state senate. It was at this time that he met Harry M. Daugherty, a behind-the-scenes political operator who became the guiding force behind the so-called Ohio Gang political machine. This group would prove instrumental in building Harding's political reputation and, later, in destroying it.

After several years in the state senate, Harding served a term as lieutenant governor. After leaving that post in 1905, he did not hold another elected office for nearly a decade, though he did try unsuccessfully to become Ohio's governor in 1910. In 1914 Harding made a run for the U.S. Senate. The Ohio Republican subsequently became one of the numerous dry congressional members that were elected that year with the assistance of the Anti-Saloon League (ASL).

Voting Dry, Drinking Wet

Like many other politicians, Harding's stance on alcohol was opportunistic and hypocritical. He was an enthusiastic drinker who loved his whiskey, yet he supported the dry platform because he knew he could win votes by doing so. Even after Prohibition was enacted, he participated in liquor-soaked poker gatherings, some of which took place at the White House during his presidency. An observer of one of these gatherings remembers the White House library being "heavy with tobacco smoke, trays with bottles containing every imaginable brand of whiskey stood about, cards and poker chips ready at hand."

Harding engaged in similar activity during his Senate career, which may explain his undistinguished record. He missed many votes and did not sponsor much legislation. He did, however, play a key role in the Prohibition debate. Harding told Wayne Wheeler of the ASL that "you fellows ought to agree to have some limitation put on the time for ratification." This suggestion was embraced by the ASL, and it brought the Prohibition resolution to a vote—the first step in its adoption.

It was the shrewd management of Harry Daugherty that made Harding the Republican presidential nominee in 1920. Daugherty championed the senator as a compromise candidate at the Republican convention, and when the other contenders failed to gain enough support, Harding got the nod. As one Republican power broker put it, "there are no first-raters this year.... Harding is the best of the second-raters."

On the campaign trail, Harding's candidacy seized the momentum and kept it. Despite his modest legislative record, Harding's "back to normalcy" slogan played well in a country that wished to put World War I behind it. He defeated Democratic candidate James M. Cox in a landslide.

Corrupt Cronies

One of Harding's best qualities was that he was likeable. An acquaintance once observed that Harding "wanted to be everybody's friend." This earned him important allies, but it also linked him to unscrupulous figures who took advantage of his trust. That was especially true once he became president. His administration was plagued by "cronyism," meaning that he placed personal friends ("cronies") in positions of power. Unfortunately, many of them turned out to be corrupt.

The most infamous example of wrongdoing was the Teapot Dome scandal that involved Albert B. Fall, the secretary of the interior. Fall allowed two oil tycoons to misappropriate naval oil reserves worth hundreds of millions of dollars. Another incident involved Colonel Charlie Forbes, one of Harding's poker pals, who was appointed health secretary. Forbes carried out a range of criminal activities in awarding contracts for supplies and hospital construction. These activities cost the government an estimated $33 million dollars while netting Forbes tens of thousands of dollars in kickbacks.

Daugherty, Harding's primary political advisor, was placed in charge of the Justice Department, which gave him authority over some aspects of Prohibition enforcement. Daugherty allowed Jess Smith, another longtime Harding associate, to have his own office in the Justice Department, though Smith had no official duties. His unofficial job was to accept payoffs. Many of them came from bootleggers who bought immunity from prosecution or assistance in obtaining permits for the production of industrial or prescription alcohol, which was used widely to create illegal liquor.

Harding himself was never directly implicated in these misdeeds, but he bears some responsibility for appointing so many dishonest officials. Because of the many scandals in his administration, he is often cited as one of the worst presidents in U.S. history. His appointees were not the only government officials to be lured by alcohol-related payoffs, but the activities of his administration certainly contributed to the general atmosphere of lawlessness that pervaded the 1920s.

A Troubled President

Harding also had personal scandals to worry about. He was involved in two different adulterous affairs that had begun before he entered the White House. One was with a married woman named Carrie Phillips and continued for five years. The other was with Nan Britton, who was just twenty years old when she met Harding in 1917. The two had a child together in 1919. These transgressions severely compromised Harding's authority when he reached the Oval Office. Both Daugherty and Smith knew of Harding's adultery, which prevented the president from taking any action against them for their illegal activities.

The president's gambling and drinking were well known in Washington and proved another liability. Wayne Wheeler eventually pressured Harding to curb these indulgences, which brought the White House parties to an end. Shortly before his death, the president told Wheeler he would give up alcohol entirely. It is unknown if he kept the promise.

By the spring of 1923 Harding had become aware of some of the criminal activities of his appointees, though these transgressions were not made public until after his death. In May 1923 Jess Smith committed suicide, leading to more speculation about wrongdoing in the administration. A month later, Harding departed on an extended tour of Alaska and the western United States. It is believed that he received more bad news about the scandals while traveling, which may have contributed to a rapid decline in his health. On July 28, he arrived in San Francisco in an exhausted state and developed bronchopneumonia. He died of a brain hemorrhage on August 2, leaving Calvin Coolidge as president.

Sources

Behr, Edward. *Prohibition: Thirteen Years That Changed America*. New York: Arcade Publishing, 1996.

Coffey, Thomas M. *The Long Thirst: Prohibition in America, 1920-1933*. New York: Norton, 1975.

Dean, John W. *Warren G. Harding*. New York: Times Books, 2004.

Kobler, John. *Ardent Spirits: The Rise and Fall of Prohibition*. New York: G. P. Putnam's Sons, 1973.

Russell, Francis. *The Shadow of Blooming Grove: Warren G. Harding in His Times*. New York: McGraw-Hill, 1968.

Charles "Lucky" Luciano (1897-1962)
Prohibition-era Mobster

Charles Luciano was born Salvatore Lucania on November 24, 1897 (some sources say November 11 or November 27) in the town of Lercara Friddi on the Italian island of Sicily. He was the third of five children born to Antonio Lucania, a sulfer miner, and his wife Rosalie (Capporelli) Lucania. Luciano grew up in poverty, and he remembered his Sicilian hometown as having "the smell of no money. The smell of being poor all the time." The family's one hope was to emigrate to the United States. When Luciano was nine years old, his mother borrowed the necessary money from a cousin, and in 1906 the family arrived in New York City.

They settled on the Lower East Side of Manhattan, where Luciano struggled with English and schoolwork. He dropped out of school at age fourteen, but not before launching his first "protection" racket: for a few pennies, he insured that Jewish children would not be beaten up on their way to and from school. Luciano and his friends idolized the neighborhood gangsters because "we knew they were rich, and rich was what counted, because the rich got away with anythin'," he recalled. After leaving school, Luciano led his own small gang of teenage criminals who specialized in muggings and robberies. He then became a courier for narcotics until 1916, when he was arrested for possession of heroin. This offense earned him a six-month stay at Hampton Farms Penitentiary.

Bootlegger on the Rise

After his release from prison, Luciano adopted a new first name—Charlie (he changed his last name from Luciana to Luciano a few years later). In the late 1910s, he began to work with several other young criminals, including Meyer Lansky, Ben "Bugsy" Siegel, and Frank Costello, who became prominent gangsters in the 1920s and 1930s. With the passage of Prohibition, these and other mobsters had a new avenue by which to increase their fortunes, and they made the most of it. Before long, Luciano had established himself as an important figure in the New York City bootleg trade.

As Luciano's power increased, he helped pioneer a new image for mobsters—stylish but understated, more reminiscent of a corporate executive than a flashy thug. His choice of residence matched the sartorial image he sought to convey: Luciano maintained a suite at the Barbizon Plaza for many years and later resided at the opulent Waldorf Towers under the name Charles Ross.

Luciano's success was closely watched by the other New York crime bosses. He received several invitations to join their organizations, and in 1927 he threw in with Giuseppe "Joe the Boss" Masseria, becoming Masseria's number two man. This move put Luciano directly in the middle of a dispute between Masseria and rival boss Salvatore Maranzano. It was a dangerous place to be. In 1929 Luciano was abducted and tortured by Maranzano's forces. The knife wounds he suffered to his face during his abduction made his right eye droop for the rest of his life. But Luciano survived the incident—or was allowed to survive it. Years later, Luciano claimed that Maranzano had overseen the torture because Luciano had refused to personally kill Masseria. The incident earned Luciano a new nickname, which was first voiced by Meyer Lansky: "That's you," Lansky remarked after he learned of his friend's brush with death, "Lucky Luciano."

After the Maranzano-Masseria feud erupted into open warfare, Luciano decided it was time to take action against the crime bosses. He orchestrated the killing of Masseria with Maranzano's okay. Then he turned on Maranzano and had him murdered. By the end of 1931, Luciano had become the most important figure in organized crime. He instituted a new "corporate" style of mob management. Each local group was allowed autonomy to run its own alcohol-related operations and other affairs, but a national commission made up of the large bosses—and chaired by Luciano—coordinated relations between the different groups. During this time, Luciano consistently emphasized the importance of cooperation and efficiency to the various syndicates. "I told 'em jealousy was our biggest enemy," Luciano remembered about one meeting of mob bosses. "In our kind of business there was so much money to be made that nobody had the right to be jealous of nobody else."

Lucky and Dewey

Luciano's prominence soon drew the attention of authorities, particularly Thomas E. Dewey, a special prosecutor named by the governor of New York to crack down on organized crime. In 1935 Dewey began to target Luciano, and the following year the gangster was indicted on charges of compulsory prostitution. To bring down Luciano, Dewey's staff had concentrated on a specific part of the Luciano empire—bordellos—and called in prostitutes, madams, and acquaintances of Luciano to tie him to the operation. In June 1936 he was convicted and sentenced to a term of thirty to fifty years in prison—the longest term ever assigned to such a crime. "It was like gettin' a life sentence," Luciano recalled when he heard the judge's decision. "Even with good behavior I'd be an old man before I got out—or maybe I'd be dead." Even in prison, however, Luciano continued to direct organized-crime operations.

After the United States entered World War II, the New York City waterfront became a center of activity in the war effort. Concerned that sabotage at the New York docks could badly hamper their operations, the Navy contacted Luciano in 1942. They asked the gangster, who controlled the harbor's Longshoremen's Union, to use his influence to ensure security along the waterfront. Luciano agreed.

Four years later, the governor of New York commuted Luciano's prison sentence, citing the gangster's cooperation in the war effort. That governor was Thomas E. Dewey—the same man who had prosecuted Luciano in 1936. Luciano later claimed that the real reason for his release was because he had paid a bribe to Dewey and agreed to support the politician in his run for governor in 1942. Whatever the reason, Luciano was released from prison under the condition that he accept deportation from the United States. On February 9, 1946, he boarded a ship in New York City harbor and set sail for Italy, the country of his birth.

Into the Old World

Luciano settled in Rome, where he continued to direct his syndicate's affairs back in the United States. In 1947 he moved to Cuba, which at that time was a haven for American organized crime outfits. Luciano saw Cuba, located just ninety miles south of Florida, as an ideal base for managing his U.S. operations. When it became known that he was on the island, however, the U.S. government pressured Cuba to deport him. Several months later, Luciano was sent back to Italy. The Italian government refused to permit him to return to Rome, so he relocated to Naples. He maintained his links to organized crime operations in the United States, but his influence weakened over time.

Luciano never married, but he lived with his Italian girlfriend Igea Lissoni until her death in 1958. In his final years, Luciano was involved in a project to make a movie based on his life. When other mobsters got wind of this, they ordered him to stop, and the movie was never made. On January 26, 1962, while meeting one of the film's producers at the Naples airport, he was stricken by a massive heart attack and died. His body was returned to New York for burial.

Sources

Burns, Ken. *Lucky Luciano: Chairman of the Mob*. DVD. A & E Entertainment, 1998.

Coffey, Thomas M. *The Long Thirst: Prohibition in America, 1920-1933*. New York: Norton, 1975.

Gosch, Martin A., and Richard Hammer. *The Last Testament of Lucky Luciano*. Boston: Little, Brown, 1974.

Bill McCoy (1877-1948)
Prohibition-era Rumrunner

William "Bill" McCoy was born in 1877 in Syracuse, New York. His father, who had previously served in the Union navy during the Civil War, was a bricklayer. During McCoy's youth, his father often regaled him with naval war stories from his Civil War service. These tales sparked a lifelong infatuation with the sea in the youngster. When the family moved to Philadelphia, McCoy was able to experience the world of ships first-hand. "I started nosing about the wharves on the Delaware [River] as instinctively as a bird dog ranges a stubble field," he later recalled. He soon became a cadet on the *Saratoga*, a school ship used to train sailors. McCoy graduated at the top of his class, then spent several years on steamships as a member of the merchant marine.

Around 1900 McCoy settled in Jacksonville, Florida, where the rest of his family was living. For the next twenty years, he and his brother Ben built boats and operated a motorboat transportation service between several cities in Florida. They did well for a time, but the arrival of motorized buses put the boat service out of business. By the time Prohibition began in 1920, the boat-building trade had also slowed. When an acquaintance approached McCoy about a new shipping enterprise, he was ready to listen.

The Honorable Tradition of Smuggling

McCoy's friend offered him $100 a day to sail a boatload of contraband liquor from the Bahamas to the United States. McCoy declined the offer, but after learning the details, he decided to get into the business for himself. McCoy and his brother sold all of the small boats they owned and used the proceeds to purchase a ninety-foot schooner, the *Henry L. Marshall*. McCoy sailed it to Nassau, in the Bahamas, and his smuggling career began.

To that point in his life, McCoy had never been a criminal, but he was able to come to terms with his new occupation. "I have precedent right out of

American history for my rum-running enterprises," he explained in Fredric Van de Water's *The Real McCoy*. He considered independence hero John Hancock to be "the patron saint of rum runners" because Hancock had smuggled liquor past customs authorities during the colonial era. Though he was not a drinker himself, McCoy disagreed with the principle of Prohibition, and for him that was reason enough to defy the ban. "Americans, since the beginnings of this nation, have always kicked holes in the laws they resented," he said.

McCoy was also attracted to rumrunning by the potential financial rewards. His first trip from the Bahamas to Georgia netted McCoy $15,000—a very large sum of money in that era. From there, his business grew. In 1921 he bought a larger schooner, the *Arethusa*, which became his pride and joy. He soon perfected the method of stationing his ships just outside the territorial waters of the United States and letting the buyers come to him, which greatly lessened his risk of arrest. This was the beginning of "rum row," which soon included hundreds of boats selling alcohol all along the eastern seaboard and in the Gulf of Mexico.

"There was money in the game," McCoy said of rumrunning, "lots of it—if you could keep it." He soon found that holding onto his riches was the hard part. After obtaining the *Arethusa*, he decided to hire another captain to sail the *Henry L. Marshall*, figuring he could double his profits. It wasn't quite that simple. In August 1921, on its first voyage without McCoy on board, the *Marshall* was seized by the Coast Guard when it strayed into U.S. waters. McCoy was ashore in Rhode Island when he heard the news. As the owner of the craft, he was indicted, but he slipped away to the city of Nassau in the Bahamas and avoided arrest.

As a wanted man, McCoy decided it was safer for him to stay in Nassau and leave the sailing to others. He added two more ships to his fleet, but they too landed in trouble thanks to their inexperienced captains. In the spring of 1922, one ship was seized. The other was badly damaged a few months later in a collision. These setbacks sapped McCoy's savings and put him on the edge of bankruptcy.

McCoy decided that he could only trust himself. With the remainder of his money, he bought a half-load of contraband liquor and personally sailed the *Arethusa* to the waters off New Jersey. He sold his cargo in two days, which solved his immediate cash-flow problem. McCoy made several more trips over the ensuing months, and by the spring of 1923 he once again ranked among the leaders of the rumrunning trade. He specialized in buying high-quality whiskey from suppliers, and unlike some rumrunners, he never "cut" (diluted) his alcohol before selling it. This decision proved a sound business strategy, for he became well-known in the industry for providing top-notch goods at fair prices.

Coast Guard Showdown

In the fall of 1923 the Coast Guard stepped up its efforts against ocean smugglers. In November, U.S. authorities instituted a new policy of searching foreign vessels outside the three-mile limit. Just as this policy went into effect, McCoy was off shore in the *Arethusa*, trying to sell the last of his liquid cargo on the final voyage of the season.

On November 24, the Coast Guard cutter *Seneca* hailed McCoy's ship, and an armed group of Coast Guardsmen boarded the *Arethusa*. The authorities had decided to test their new policy on rum row's most famous captain. After a tense standoff, McCoy agreed to follow the Coast Guard ship into port. As they made their way in, however, McCoy made a final run for freedom. The Coast Guard responded by firing its cannons at the fleeing *Arethusa*. After several near misses, McCoy decided not to risk his life or those of his crew. He turned back and surrendered to the Coast Guard vessel. His days as a rumrunner were finished.

McCoy received a nine-month jail sentence, but he passed most of the time in comfort. A corrupt warden allowed him to stay in a hotel for part of his sentence, and during this time he was free to come and go as he pleased. Upon his release in December 1925, he returned to Florida, where he lived for the rest of his life. He was left with fond memories of his days as a rumrunner. "There was all the kick of gambling and the thrill of sport, and, besides these, there were the open sea and the boom of the wind against full sails, dawn coming out of the ocean, and nights under the rocking stars," he recalled in *The Real McCoy*. "These caught and held me most of all."

McCoy also retired with a significant bundle of money from his rumrunning days. He later claimed that legal fees exhausted most of his savings, but he was able to live comfortably for the rest of his life without working. He died on December 30, 1948, in Stuart, Florida.

Sources

Coffey, Thomas M. *The Long Thirst: Prohibition in America, 1920-1933*. New York: Norton, 1975.

Halifax Historical Museum. "Bill McCoy: 1877-1948." http://www.halifaxhistorical.org/mccoy.htm (accessed July 2004).

Van de Water, Frederic F. *The Real McCoy*. Garden City, NY: Doubleday, Doran, 1931.

Carry Nation (1846-1911)
Prohibition activist

Born Carry Amelia Moore on November 25, 1846, in Garrard County, Kentucky, Nation was the daughter of George Moore and Mary (Campbell) Moore. Insanity was a common trait in her family. Her mother suffered from delusions that she was Queen Victoria, and Nation's grandmother, aunt, uncle, and cousin—all on her mother's side—also experienced dementia. Moore's father was a livestock dealer and planter who was a member of a religious organization called the Disciples of Christ. He also owned slaves, and Nation spent a lot of time in their company, absorbing African American folklore and spirituality. At age ten, she underwent a religious conversion and thereafter claimed to have frequent conversations with Jesus. She would later cite her Christian beliefs as the basis of her anti-saloon activity, describing herself as "a bulldog, running along at the feet of Jesus, barking at what He doesn't like."

The family prospered for a time, but the Civil War brought an end to their good fortune and forced them to move west. In the mid-1860s, the Moores settled in Belton, Missouri. Nation's schooling had been intermittent up to that point, but she eventually earned a teaching certificate from the State Normal School in Warrensburg, Missouri.

Personal Tragedies Fuel Temperance Beliefs

In Belton, Nation met a doctor named Charles Gloyd. They were married in 1867, but it was not a happy union. Gloyd was an alcoholic, and his drinking eventually forced Nation to return to her parents. She was pregnant at the time of her separation from Gloyd, and after returning to her parents' home she gave birth to a daughter named Charlien. Gloyd drank himself to death six months after the child was born. Nation's disastrous first marriage thus transformed her into an ardent temperance activist.

After appealing to God for another husband, she met David Nation, a minister in the Christian Church who was nineteen years older than Carry. They were married in 1877. More misfortune followed. Charlien suffered from an affliction that caused the skin of her cheek to rot away. She survived the ordeal but remained in poor physical and mental health. She eventually ended up in an insane asylum. Nation and her husband struggled through a variety of jobs, including farming and operating hotels, but they barely earned enough to survive. They moved frequently, living in different parts of Missouri, Texas, and Kansas.

By the late 1890s Carry and David Nation had settled in Medicine Lodge, Kansas. The town supported several saloons that operated in open violation of the state's constitutional amendment outlawing alcohol. Nation helped form a local branch of the Women's Christian Temperance Union (WCTU). The chapter conducted demonstrations against the saloons and eventually drove them out of business. With the closure of the saloons, the only remaining business in Medicine Lodge that dispensed alcohol was a drug store. Determined to stamp out this lingering threat to the town's sobriety, Nation marched into the drugstore one day in 1899 and used a sledgehammer to smash a keg of whiskey. The druggist soon left Medicine Lodge, giving the WCTU a complete victory.

In June 1900 Nation proclaimed that she heard a voice telling her to "go to Kiowa," a nearby town loaded with saloons. Nation arrived with a buggy full of bricks, rocks, and bottles. She marched into a watering hole and told the owner "get out of the way. I don't want to strike you, but I am going to break up this den of vice." She then kept her promise, hurling pieces of brick that shattered the bar's mirror and bottles. She entered two more saloons on the same day and destroyed them in the same fashion. She was finally apprehended, but the authorities later released her since the drinking establishments were operating illegally. Nation returned to Medicine Lodge and bought a hatchet at the hardware store. Then she rode out once more in search of other saloons to smite.

Hatchetation All across the Nation

Nation's first stop was Wichita, where she used her hatchet on two saloons and twice attacked an upscale hotel bar. She was jailed briefly for her Wichita escapades, and photographs of her kneeling in prayer in her jail cell appeared in papers across the country. After gaining her release, she took her campaign of destruction—which she termed "hatchetation"—to other Kansas towns, including Topeka, Enterprise, and Leavenworth. She ignored her husband's requests to return home, and he eventually divorced her on the grounds of abandonment.

Next, Nation looked beyond the state's borders. She staged surprise attacks all around the eastern half of the United States. Marching into saloons in such far-flung cities as Des Moines, Cincinnati, Atlantic City, and Philadelphia armed only with her hatchet and her righteous anger, she left piles of splintered wood and broken glass in her wake. Even worldly New York City seemed to tremble before her. Some Big Apple bars temporarily locked their doors when she arrived in town, and saloon owner John L. Sullivan, a former heavyweight boxing champion, refused to meet Nation face to face.

Sullivan's reluctance was understandable. Even at fifty-four, the age when she began her violent campaign, Nation was an imposing person. She stood about six feet tall, weighed 175 pounds, and carried ample muscle and a grim look of determination. She occasionally encountered saloon owners who tried to stop her by force, but most were too shocked or too scared to do more than watch the carnage unfold. As always, she was driven by her sense of righteousness, which was expressed in her fighting words: "Smash! Smash! For Jesus's sake, smash!"

Nation was jailed thirty times, but she always returned to action once she had paid her fine or served her sentence. In some cases she received legal and financial assistance from the WCTU and other supporters. Despite this support, the WCTU was of two minds about Nation's tactics. The organization's *Union Signal* publication noted that "Mrs. Nation's hatchet has done more to frighten the liquor sellers and awaken the sleeping consciences of Kansas voters than the entire official force of the state has heretofore done." But ultimately the WCTU disavowed Nation, deciding that her "lawless methods" caused "more harm than good."

Success and Ridicule

Nation's anti-saloon crusade made her a coast-to-coast sensation. As time passed, she kept herself in the public eye by making anti-alcohol speeches and by publishing a newspaper, *The Smasher's Mail*. Her notoriety undoubtedly brought the temperance movement a lot of attention and helped publicize the negative aspects of the saloons. In some areas, her campaign led to increased enforcement of existing liquor laws.

But fame became a double-edged sword. After a time, many Americans came to see her more as a source of amusement than a serious reformer. She was frequently lampooned in newspaper cartoons, and saloon owners got in on the fun by posting signs that read "all nations served ... except Carry." Nation's own actions contributed to her increasingly silly reputation. She sold souvenir hatchets to raise money and appeared as a feature attraction at fairs and carnivals, in which she sometimes re-enacted saloon assaults for snickering audiences.

In her final years, Nation was able to buy a farm in the Ozark Mountains, where she spent much of her time. In January 1911 she suffered a nervous collapse after a lecture in Arkansas. She spent her final months in a mental hospital at Leavenworth, Kansas. She died there on June 2, 1911.

Sources
Asbury, Herbert. *The Great Illusion: An Informal History of Prohibition*. Garden City, NY: Doubleday & Company, 1950.
Behr, Edward. *Prohibition: Thirteen Years That Changed America*. New York: Arcade Publishing, 1996.
Grace, Fran. *Carry A. Nation: Retelling the Life*. Bloomington: Indiana University Press, 2004.
Kobler, John. *Ardent Spirits: The Rise and Fall of Prohibition*. New York: G. P. Putnam's Sons, 1973.
Taylor, Robert Lewis. *Vessel of Wrath: The Life and Times of Carry Nation*. New York: New American Library, 1966.

George Remus (c. 1876-1952)
Prohibition-era Bootlegger

George Remus was born in Germany around 1876. Around the age of four or five, he immigrated to the United States with his parents, Maria (Karg) Remus and Franck Remus. In Germany, George's father had been a weaver, but after the family settled in Milwaukee, he took a job in the lumber industry. When George was fourteen, his father was stricken with articular rheumatism and was unable to work. The family moved to Chicago, where George quit school and became the main breadwinner. He worked in his uncle's drugstore for five years, then, at age nineteen, he bought the store himself and earned his pharmacist's license. He soon added a second store and also became an optometrist. He then began taking law classes at night, and by the time he was in his mid-twenties, he had begun a new career as a lawyer. Remus married in the late 1890s and had a daughter, but the marriage came to an end in the late 1910s after he became romantically involved with Imogene Holmes, who worked as his legal secretary.

Remus became a successful defense lawyer in Chicago, pulling in $50,000 per year, a healthy sum in that era. Some of his clients were mobsters (Johnny Torrio, for instance), so Remus paid close attention to the Volstead Act when it became law in 1919. After studying its finer points, he concluded that it was time to undertake yet another career. He sold his law practice and moved to Cincinnati, Ohio, with Holmes. He chose his new hometown because it was close to the majority of the country's whiskey distilleries and bonded warehouses. With $100,000 in savings to finance him, Remus made his entrance into the world of bootlegging.

The House That Prohibition Built

Remus soon took ownership of the biggest whiskey distilleries in the country, and he also founded a series of drug companies to sell medicinal alcohol. His drug companies bought whiskey from his distilleries. They sold some of that whiskey legitimately, supplying pharmacists who filled doctor's prescriptions. But a far greater share of the whiskey went to the illegal market—speakeasies, mobsters, and private buyers.

Remus developed an elaborate organization. A storage and bottling facility known as Death Valley Farm was established outside of Cincinnati. A fleet of delivery trucks shipped the booze throughout the Midwest, their trips made safe by stacks of bribery money. "Remus was to bootlegging what Rockefeller was to oil," wrote Paul Y. Anderson in the St. Louis *Post-Dispatch*. "In the sheer imagination of his plan, in the insolent sweep of his ambition and power … Remus can bear comparison with the captains of industry."

Like the industrial tycoons of the era, Remus embraced an opulent lifestyle. He bought a thirty-one-room mansion in Cincinnati and had it totally renovated. The Olympic-size swimming pool cost $100,000 by itself. By this time Remus and Holmes had married, and the couple staged elaborate parties at the mansion as a way of gaining entrance into the world of the social elite. At one such gathering, Remus reportedly presented each of the fifty women in attendance with a brand-new car. Some scholars believe that F. Scott Fitzgerald modeled the affluent, party-throwing title character of *The Great Gatsby* after Remus.

In October 1921 two out-of-state Prohibition directors, Sam Collins and Burt Morgan, engineered a raid on Death Valley Farm. Though Remus had paid tens of thousands of dollars in bribes to ensure that he would not see prison time, his protection failed him. He was sentenced to two years behind bars for alcohol violations and received a separate one-year sentence in Ohio for "maintaining a nuisance" at the Death Valley Farm. The convictions were an undeniable setback, but Remus remained free to continue his bootlegging activities while the sentences were appealed. In June 1923 he partnered with several other investors to buy the Jack Daniel's distillery in St. Louis.

After exhausting his appeals, Remus began serving his jail term in Atlanta in January 1924. Meanwhile, his criminal enterprise continued. Before departing, he had given his wife power of attorney over his affairs so that she could make necessary payments to keep the bootlegging operation afloat. He also asked her to seek out a Justice Department agent named Franklin N. Dodge. Remus had learned that, for the right price, Dodge might be able to secure a pardon for the bootlegger. Imogene Remus arranged a meeting with Dodge and found that Remus's information was correct. Unfortunately for the bootlegger, the meeting between the agent and his wife sparked an adulterous affair.

The Bootlegger Betrayed

Dodge subsequently left the Justice Department and conspired with Imogene Remus to disappear with her husband's bootlegging fortune. While Remus remained in prison, his wife used her power-of-attorney to empty bank accounts and sell off many of the distilleries. She also removed the valuable paintings and furnishings from their mansion. Two days before his release from the Atlanta prison in 1925, Remus was notified that his wife wanted a divorce. He returned home to find the Cincinnati house almost completely empty.

Imogene's plotting didn't end there. She and Dodge also sought to have Remus deported on the grounds that he had never become a U.S. citizen. This was untrue, and nothing ever came of their efforts. Later, she allegedly tried to hire hit men to murder Remus.

Not surprisingly, his wife's betrayal infuriated Remus. In May 1926, Remus began serving his Ohio jail term. Upon his release a year later, he returned to Cincinnati. His bootlegging empire was no more, and his savings were nearly exhausted. Meanwhile, Imogene's divorce proceedings were still pending. A court date was set for early October. Remus waited and plotted.

On the morning of October 6, 1927, Remus ordered his chauffeur to drive him to the Cincinnati hotel where his wife was staying. When she departed in a cab, Remus directed the chauffeur to follow. A short time later, Remus's driver forced the cab to stop by the side of the road. Remus strode to the cab and shot his wife in the stomach, disregarding her protests. He turned himself into the police a short time later. When notified that his wife had died from the attack, he expressed no remorse. "I'm happy," he said. "This is the first peace of mind I've had in two years."

The murder trial was a sensational affair that attracted media from all across the country. Remus was allowed to defend himself, though another lawyer handled many of the courtroom proceedings. His defense was temporary insanity. Evidence of Imogene's treachery was introduced during the trial, and one witness testified that she had offered him money to kill Remus.

On December 20, 1927, the bootlegger was found not guilty by reason of insanity. The prosecution managed to have Remus committed to an Ohio insane asylum, but his stay there was brief. After being declared sane, he was released on June 20, 1928.

Prohibition was still the law of the land when Remus gained his release, but he turned his back on the world of bootlegging. Instead, he opted to work in a legitimate field—patent medicine. Later, he turned his hand to real estate. He sold his mansion and led a quieter and less opulent life, marrying for a third time. He died on January 20, 1952.

Sources

Behr, Edward. *Prohibition: Thirteen Years That Changed America*. New York: Arcade Publishing, 1996.
Coffey, Thomas M. *The Long Thirst: Prohibition in America, 1920-1933*. New York: Norton, 1975.
Kobler, John. *Ardent Spirits: The Rise and Fall of Prohibition*. New York: G. P. Putnam's Sons, 1973.

Al Smith (1873-1944)
Anti-Prohibition Governor of New York and Democratic Presidential Candidate

Alfred Emanuel Smith was born December 30, 1873, in New York City. His father, also named Alfred Emanuel Smith, delivered goods by horse-drawn wagon. His mother was Catherine (Mulvehill) Smith. Both of Smith's parents were second-generation Americans from Europe. His mother's parents were Irish; his father's heritage was Italian and German. Smith grew up on the Lower East Side of Manhattan, a crowded immigrant district during his childhood.

Smith's father died in 1886 after several years of poor health. This forced Smith, then in the seventh grade, to drop out of school to help support the family. He was employed as an office boy and clerk, among other jobs. An outgoing youth, Smith made a lot of friends, including many that he met through the Catholic church he attended. This eventually drew him into the orbit of the political power brokers in his neighborhood. These connections landed Smith a job as a process server and lifted him to a seat in the New York Assembly in 1904. In 1900 he married Catherine Dunn, with whom he eventually had five children.

The Tammany Man

Smith owed his political career to the backing of the Tammany Hall political machine. The Tammany group had originated in the late 1700s, and by the mid-1800s had become quite powerful in New York City. The Tammany leadership drew on immigrants for much of its support, and saloon owners often organized support for the Tammany candidates. In the late nineteenth century the group was plagued by scandal, but it remained an influential force in American politics. By the time Smith became a politician, its corrupt practices had been curbed somewhat, but it was still closely identified with the political abuses that helped inspire Prohibition and other attempts at reform.

During his time in the New York legislature in Albany, Smith received direction from Tammany boss Charles Murphy. But he also charted his own course, promoting many progressive reforms. He was especially active after the 1911 Triangle Waist Company fire in New York City, in which 141 people were killed. Most of the victims were immigrant women who worked in the garment factory where the fire broke out. After the tragedy, Smith sponsored a bill to create a workplace investigation committee and later sponsored worker-friendly legislation that helped curb dangerous industrial hazards and instituted progressive wage, workmen's compensation, and work week regulations. In 1913 Smith reached the peak of power in the legislature, becoming the speaker of the assembly. This leadership position gave Smith ample opportunity to display his oratorical skills, sharp political instincts, and public poise. Two years later he gave up his office, and in 1918 he was elected as the state's governor. He was voted out in the nationwide Republican sweep of 1920, but Smith battled back to win the governor's office in 1922 and was reelected in 1924 and 1926.

An Opponent of Prohibition

As governor of New York, Smith emerged as one of the nation's leading critics of Prohibition. In 1920 he complained that the Eighteenth Amendment had been "imposed upon a hundred million free people, without asking their direct consent," and he maintained that it was "a restriction to their personal liberty." Further, he believed that the Volstead Act was "a dishonest and hypocritical interpretation of the Eighteenth Amendment." He argued that it should be modified to allow the sale of beer with 2.75 percent alcohol.

Smith personally enjoyed drinking alcohol, and Prohibition did not change his tastes. He kept a supply of liquor in the governor's mansion, and was known to speak fondly of drink when he thought his comments were off the record. On a warm day in 1923, Smith asked a group of reporters, "wouldn't you like to have your foot on the rail and blow the foam off some suds?"

During Smith's second term as governor he was forced to face the Prohibition issue directly. Previously, New York had passed the Mullan-Gage Act, which empowered state officials to pursue and prosecute those who violated Prohibition. In 1923, after opposition to the Eighteenth Amendment had grown, the state legislature passed a law that repealed the Mullan-Gage Act. After much hand wringing, Smith signed the bill into law. He offered a detailed justification for his actions, but it did little to change his political image: he became known as a wet who wished to do away with Prohibition. Critics charged that he had failed to uphold the U.S. Constitution. This image did not hurt Smith much when he sought reelection as governor, but it proved damaging when he set his sights on a higher political office.

Smith was a contender for the Democratic nomination for president in 1924, but so was William Gibbs McAdoo. The party split between the two, with the wet Catholic wing of Democrats in the Northeast supporting Smith and the dry, heavily Protestant Democrats of the South and West backing McAdoo. Neither man could get the necessary backing for nomination, so a compromise candidate, John W. Davis, became the nominee. The divided Democrats fared poorly in the 1924 elections, and Davis was soundly defeated by Republican President Calvin Coolidge.

Pursuing the Presidency

In 1928 the Democratic Party was eager to avoid a split in its ranks. Presenting a unified front was made easier by the fact that the dry, rural Democrats had no viable candidate to rally around. Smith easily won the party's nomination, overcoming anti-Catholic bigotry from some Protestant Democrats to become first Roman Catholic candidate for president for a major political party.

During this time, Smith continued to voice his opposition to Prohibition. He sent a telegram to the political convention stating that "Democratic principles of local state government and states' rights" were the solution to the alcohol problem. In other words, he favored repeal of the Eighteenth Amendment, which was a federal measure.

This position stoked outright rebellion from some factions of Smith's own party. Southern dry Democrats led by Bishop James Cannon Jr. of the Anti-Saloon League came out in opposition to Smith. The election campaign also was marred by scurrilous rumors about Smith. These tales, disseminated by his political opponents, included stories of drunken behavior and suggestions that, if elected, he would turn a portion of the White House over to the Pope for use as his American office. Smith spoke out strongly against the "bigotry, hatred, intolerance, and un-American sectarian division" used against him, and his platform emphasized socially progressive policy goals. At election time, though, Smith failed to expand his support beyond Northern urban centers, and he even lost his home state of New York. Republican candidate Herbert Hoover won by a wide margin.

The defeat signaled the end of Smith's career as an elected politician. He tried to serve as an advisor to Franklin D. Roosevelt, who—with Smith's backing—had taken over as New York governor. Roosevelt distanced himself from Smith, however, and the two became rivals. Smith turned to the private sector, becoming president of the corporation that built the Empire State Building. He made a serious bid for the Democratic presidential nomination in 1932, but was beaten by Roosevelt.

Smith began to espouse more conservative views in the mid-1930s, becoming a vocal critic of Roosevelt's presidency and branding the New Deal as a form of socialism. These views led him to break with the Democratic Party in 1936, and they were a source of puzzlement to friends and colleagues who had admired his progressive record as governor of New York. Smith suffered from lung, heart, and liver troubles in later years, and he died on October 4, 1944.

Sources

Coffey, Thomas M. *The Long Thirst: Prohibition in America, 1920-1933*. New York: Norton, 1975.

Eldot, Paula. *Governor Alfred E. Smith: The Politician as Reformer*. New York: Garland, 1983.

Finan, Christopher M. *Alfred E. Smith: The Happy Warrior*. New York: Hill and Wang, 2002.

Josephson, Matthew, and Hannah Josephson. *Al Smith: Hero of the Cities*. Boston: Houghton-Mifflin, 1969.

Slayton, Robert A. *Empire Statesman: The Rise and Redemption of Al Smith*. New York: Free Press, 2001.

Billy Sunday (1862-1935)
Christian Evangelist and Anti-alcohol Crusader

William Ashley Sunday was born November 19, 1862, near Ames, Iowa. The same year that he was born, his father, also named William Sunday, enlisted in the Union Army. He died a few months later of pneumonia. His mother, Mary Jane (Corey) Sunday, raised her three children by herself for several years, then remarried. Sunday's childhood was marked by misfortune. Unable to get along with his stepfather, he moved in with his grandparents. His oldest brother, Albert, was kicked in the head by a horse and suffered brain damage. His half sister was burned to death in a bonfire accident. Both he and his brother Edward spent several years in an orphanage, probably because of financial hardship.

At age fourteen, Sunday struck out on his own, working at several jobs. After being taken in by a kindly family in Nevada, Iowa, he was able to complete high school. He played on a local baseball team, then was hired as a professional in 1883 by the Chicago Whitestockings. His career lasted for nine seasons, during which time he worked as a locomotive fireman in the off-season.

Rising Star in American Evangelism

Before and during his years in professional baseball, Sunday had a reputation for fighting, womanizing, and drinking. In 1886, however, he underwent a religious conversion that was partly inspired by a woman in whom he developed a romantic interest. "She was Presbyterian, so I am Presbyterian," he later explained. "If she had been a Catholic, I would have been a Catholic—because I was hot on the trail of Nell." In 1888 Helen "Nell" Thompson became his wife, and they later had four children.

In 1891 Sunday gave up baseball and began working for the Young Men's Christian Association (YMCA), where he performed evangelical work in saloons and on street corners. He then took a job as an administrator and publicist for traveling evangelist J. Wilbur Chapman. In 1896 Chapman went into temporary retirement and Sunday began conducting his own revival meetings.

Sunday's early revivals were well received but rather conventional in content and format. In the early years of the 1900s, however, Sunday began incorporating more entertainment into his presentations. Instead of a single singer/organist, he employed full bands and large choirs—by 1904 his show featured 300 singers. The biggest draw, however, was Sunday himself. He abandoned the quiet, respectable style of his early years and instead became "God's mouthpiece"—a dramatic showman who climbed atop chairs, threw off his collar and coat, shouted and gestured. In short, he was as much an entertainer as he was a preacher. One newspaper reported that "Sunday had imitated nearly everybody and everything in the whole gamut of stage acting" during one sermon, "even in diving off the stage and coming up blowing water out of his lungs in imitation of a man diving after a pearl."

Sunday also learned to tailor his language and message to his audience. In the beginning, his revivals usually took place in the small farming communities of the Midwest. By interjecting homespun humor and popular slang into his talks, he connected with the crowds. Sunday played to their prejudices as well, making fun of large cities and high culture. His religious message was fundamentalist in nature: he upheld conservative values and the authority of the Bible, denouncing modern trends and scientific thought. This was especially true of Charles Darwin's theory of evolution, which he rejected outright: "If you mean by evolution that I came from a monkey, good night!"

A Fierce Enemy of Alcohol

The topic dearest to Sunday's heart was alcohol's corrosive impact on American families and institutions. His most famous speech was the so-called "Booze Sermon," a blend of standard talking points and inspired improvisation. This fiery oration proclaimed the saloon to be the gravest problem facing mankind. "The saloon is the sum of all villainies," he declared. "It is worse than war or pestilence. It is the crime of crimes. It is the parent of crimes and the mother of sins…. And to license such an incarnate fiend of hell is the dirtiest, low-down, damnable business on top of this old earth."

Sunday's lengthy speech alternated between humor, pathos, and anger. He objected to alcohol on moral grounds, but he spent a lot of time emphasizing its impact on familial health: "It will take the last bucket of coal out of your cellar, and the last cent out of your pocket, and will send you home bleary-eyed and staggering to your wife and children." Sunday also condemned alcohol as a threat to civilized society. "It cocks the highwayman's pistol. It puts the rope in the hands of the mob. It is the anarchist of the world," he declared. "It sent the bullet through the body of Lincoln.... Every plot that was ever hatched against the government and law, was born and bred, and crawled out of the grog-shop to damn this country."

Sunday beseeched his audiences to take action against the saloons in their midst. These exhortations frequently resulted in civic action against the bars as soon as Sunday's revival came to a close. His orations proved instrumental in whipping up anti-alcohol sentiment between 1900 and 1920, especially in the rural heartland that became the foundation of the Prohibition movement.

America's Leading Revival Preacher

There were two measures of success for traveling evangelists, and Sunday excelled at both. First, his rallies inspired large numbers of people to accept Jesus. The evangelist developed a dramatic method of calling forth the newly saved, having them come to the front of the meeting space to grasp his hand. Second, he raised a lot of money in donations. This was crucial to the viability of the revivals, because the money collected from attendees paid the expenses of staging the event, travel costs, and the salaries of Sunday and his crew. These collections helped make the evangelist a millionaire.

Sunday's fame grew throughout the 1910s. He expanded beyond the Midwest "corn belt" and began presenting high-profile revivals in large cities. He reached the peak of his popularity in 1917, when he completed a seventy-one day revival in New York City that was staged in an immense 20,000-seat tabernacle. More than 1.4 million people attended, and his ministry reported that more than 98,000 attendees experienced a religious conversion during the revival.

The passage of Prohibition two years later was another crowning achievement for Sunday, but its failure proved disillusioning for the evangelist. The 1920s also saw his popularity fade in the northern United States, especially in the large cities. As a result, he concentrated on the South, where his fundamentalist message was better received. During this period his sermons became more extreme and reactionary, promoting a specific type of Americanism that excluded those who were not native-born fundamentalist Christians.

With the coming of the Depression and the repeal of Prohibition, Sunday became pessimistic about the future. His sermons began dwelling on the end of the world as foretold in the Bible. He suffered a serious heart attack while on stage in 1933 but managed to recover. The following year he predicted that the apocalypse would take place in 1935. Sunday died on November 6, 1935, after suffering his second heart attack in six months.

Sources

Bruns, Roger A. *Preacher: Billy Sunday and Big-Time American Evangelism*. New York: W.W. Norton, 1992.

Ellis, William T. *Billy Sunday: The Man and His Message*. n.p., c. 1914.

McLoughlin, William G., Jr. *Billy Sunday Was His Real Name*. Chicago: University of Chicago Press, 1955.

Wayne B. Wheeler (1869-1927)
General Counsel and National Legislative Super-intendent of the Anti-Saloon League

Wayne Bidwell Wheeler was born November 10, 1869, near Brook-field, Ohio. He was the third of four children born to Joseph Wheeler, a live-stock dealer, and Ursula (Hutchinson) Wheel-er. Because his father's business frequently kept him away from home, Wayne assumed a lot of responsibility on the Wheeler farm at a young age. One day a drunken field hand acci-dentally stabbed Wheeler in the leg with a pitchfork, an incident that gave the boy a painful lesson in the dangers of drink.

After completing high school, Wheeler worked for two years as a teacher so that he could earn tuition money for college. In 1890 he enrolled at Oberlin College in Oberlin, Ohio. Wheeler's choice of schools proved fateful. The college was already a center for temperance activity, and in 1893 Reverend Howard Hyde Russell founded the Anti-Saloon League of Ohio at Oberlin. Wheeler was in his third year of school at the time, and Rus-sell's work inspired him to become a speech-making temperance activist. "The simplicity and practical nature of the new organization captured me," Wheeler later wrote. Upon Wheeler's graduation in 1894, Russell offered him a full-time position with the Anti-Saloon League of Ohio.

The Driving Wheel

Wheeler became famous for his tireless efforts to organize opposition to wet candidates. Outfitted with a bicycle, he pedaled through Ohio's rural counties, soliciting support from religious leaders. His first major success was in engineering the defeat of John Locke, a prominent state politician who had opposed a local-option bill. Wheeler convinced a well-known businessman to stand against Locke, then organized support for his candidate in area church-es. Afterward, the league trumpeted the news: "Who defeated Locke? Wheel-er and his wheel."

In the mid-1890s, the Ohio chapter's lack of legal expertise prompted Wheeler to pursue a law degree. In 1898 he received his degree from Case Reserve University in Cleveland and became the chapter's attorney. In this position he participated in thousands of alcohol-related trials, helped draft legislation, and promoted dry candidates and issues with great success.

In 1901 Wheeler married Ella Belle Candy of Columbus, Ohio. They had three children, but family life did not divert Wheeler from his anti-alcohol work. Throughout his career he generally worked fifteen to eighteen hours a day. Justin Steuart, Wheeler's publicity secretary and later his biographer, wrote in *Wayne Wheeler: Dry Boss* that "home, family, friendships, pleasures ... all of these meant nothing to him beside the consuming passion for the cause." Wheeler also had a passion for power, and in 1903 he assumed the Ohio chapter's senior post of state superintendent. The following year he helped elect a dry Democrat as governor, overcoming Ohio's historic allegiance to the Republican Party.

Fighting for National Prohibition

After the league officially called for national Prohibition in 1913, Wheeler became active in the fight for the Eighteenth Amendment. He did double duty for a time, serving as both the Ohio superintendent and as senior attorney for the ASL's national organization. In 1916 he gave up his Ohio post and relocated to Washington, D.C., where he became the ASL's general counsel. He later added the title of legislative superintendent.

Wheeler enjoyed significant input on the different drafts of the Prohibition amendment and guided its final wording. One of his additions was the "concurrent power" passage that later caused enforcement problems because some state officials interpreted it to mean that they did not have to take an active role in enforcing Prohibition. Wheeler was even more instrumental in the creation of the Volstead Act. It is generally accepted that he wrote the bill himself and that Congressman Volstead made only minor changes to it. The fact that a non-elected lobbyist drafted a federal law raised some controversy, but it did not prevent the bill's passage.

Wheeler's influence over the shape of the key Prohibition statutes signaled his rise to power in the ASL. He never held organization's senior position—general superintendent—but by the early 1920s he was widely regarded as the person who exercised the most authority over the league's activities. Steuart, for example, ventured that "Wheeler seemed to be the only person in the country who was sure just what the Volstead Act meant and how it should be enforced." This knowledge, coupled with his political power, led law enforcement officials to seek his counsel throughout the Prohibition era.

Dry Boss

Wheeler's input expanded into many other areas. He effectively ruled the Prohibition Unit for several years by placing Roy Haynes, his handpicked candidate, in the commissioner's office. He also applied the league's political leverage brilliantly in Congress during the 1920s. His frequent pronouncements on Prohibition were taken as the official position of the ASL and of the dry lobby in general. Above all else, Wheeler became one of the nation's premier political power brokers.

As the nation's leading architect of Prohibition, though, Wheeler also bears some blame for Prohibition's shortcomings. While enforcement of Prohibition would have been difficult under any circumstances, Wheeler's Volstead Act created a range of problems, including unseemly political patronage, official corruption, and inefficient bureaucracy. In addition, his choice of Roy Haynes as the federal government's point man on Prohibition enforcement proved unwise. This led to a major political loss for Wheeler when General Lincoln C. Andrews took over many of Haynes's duties in 1925. Two years later, Haynes was forced out of office completely, despite Wheeler's strenuous objections.

Though he faced increased resistance to his Prohibition agenda in the mid-1920s, it was health rather than politics that proved Wheeler's undoing. By 1926, he was suffering from serious heart and kidney ailments, perhaps brought on by his relentless work schedule. Finally, in 1927, he took a prolonged vacation at his Michigan cottage to try and recover his strength. During his time off, tragedy struck. A gasoline stove exploded in the cottage, fatally burning Ella Belle Wheeler. Wheeler's father in law, who was visiting at the time, witnessed his daughter in flames and suffered a fatal heart attack. Wheeler was uninjured in the explosion, but the loss of his wife was a final blow. A few months later he was hospitalized in Battle Creek, Michigan, where he died of a heart attack on September 5, 1927.

Sources
Behr, Edward. *Prohibition: Thirteen Years That Changed America*. New York: Arcade Publishing, 1996.
Kerr, K. Austin. *Organized for Prohibition: A New History of the Anti-Saloon League*. New Haven: Yale University Press, 1985.
Kobler, John. *Ardent Spirits: The Rise and Fall of Prohibition*. New York: G. P. Putnam's Sons, 1973.
Steuart, Justin. *Wayne Wheeler: Dry Boss*. New York: Fleming H. Revell Company, 1928.

Mabel Walker Willebrandt (1889-1963)
Director of Prohibition Enforcement in the Justice Department

Born Mabel Elizabeth Walker on May 23, 1889, Willebrandt was the daughter of David William Walker and Myrtle S. (Eaton) Walker. Her parents worked as teachers and operated several small-town newspapers. The family lived in several different locations in Missouri and Kansas, struggling to make a living in frontier farm settlements. Willebrandt was educated at home until the age of thirteen, then attended a formal school after the family moved to Kansas City in 1902. In 1906 she began studies at Park Academy in Parkville, Missouri, but was forced to leave the college after a heated debate of religious issues with the president.

Willebrandt returned to her family and accompanied them to northern Michigan. After settling there, Willebrandt taught school and attended college classes at Ferris Institute in Big Rapids. In 1910 she married Arthur F. Willebrandt, and the couple moved to Arizona so that Arthur could recover from a bout with tuberculosis. Willebrandt graduated from the Tempe Normal School the following year, and then she and her husband moved again, this time to the Los Angeles area. Willebrandt taught school in the daytime and studied law in the evenings at the University of Southern California. In 1916 she received her law degree, and the same year she and her husband separated. Their divorce became final in 1924.

While still a law student, Willebrandt began working for a police court defender's office, assisting women who had been charged with crimes such as prostitution. She argued more than 2,000 cases as a public defender in the late 1910s. She also opened her own successful private practice, handling business, real-estate, and personal-injury cases.

Going to Washington

Willebrandt had inherited her political views from her Republican father and aligned herself with the party's progressive wing. As the Prohibition era began, her political beliefs brought her a new opportunity. In 1921 the Republican administration of Warren G. Harding took power in Washington, D.C. Harding's predecessor, Woodrow Wilson, had broken new ground by appointing a woman to the position of assistant attorney general. Harding was eager to continue this tradition because he saw it as a way to curry favor with female voters (women's suffrage had just been enacted). With backing from key California Republicans, Willebrandt got the nod, and in August 1921 she moved to Washington, D.C.

Just thirty-two years of age when the took the Justice Department job, Willebrandt later admitted that "I was a young lawyer, much *too* young when appointed, for the responsibilities heaped on me." Willebrandt had jurisdiction over prisons, income and estate taxes, and several other areas, but her duties related to Prohibition enforcement are what put her in the public eye. She had no previous track record as a prohibitionist. She later conceded that "while it was legal to do so, I had liquor in my own home in California, and used it, in moderation, of course." With the Eighteenth Amendment now a part of the Constitution, however, she vowed to obey and uphold Prohibition.

Well aware that many U.S. attorneys had been corrupted by payoffs, Willebrandt established a special "flying squadron" of attorneys to carry out prosecutions when other Justice Department personnel were unable to get the job done. She also coordinated complex operations to bring down important violators. In 1922, she scored her first big victory by orchestrating the investigation and prosecution of a large alcohol smuggling ring in Savannah, Georgia. Other successful prosecutions followed, including the convictions of five large-scale bootleggers in Mobile, Alabama. Cincinnati alcohol kingpin George Remus, who Willebrandt described as "the most notorious and defiant bootlegger," also endured jail time as a direct result of the efforts of Willebrandt and her investigators.

On the public relations front, Willebrandt spoke out on the need for strict enforcement in lectures and magazine articles. She pleaded with citizens to obey the law and to cooperate with enforcement. "Let us pull together," she wrote in *The Woman Citizen*. "You catch the little fellow, punish him quickly and drastically, and then hold us in the Federal Government responsible if we do not mobilize every agency of the Government to dam up the sources of illicit wholesale supply."

Political Controversy

Willebrandt's ardent support of Prohibition was generally respected, but she became embroiled in several political dust-ups that earned her negative publicity. Two of them occurred during the 1928 presidential campaign. Willebrandt supported Herbert Hoover, the Republican nominee, which placed her in opposition to Democrat Al Smith, governor of New York. The same week that Smith received the Democratic nomination, she ordered a large-scale raid on speakeasies throughout Smith's hometown of New York City. This led to allegations that she had staged the raids to make Smith look bad at a crucial moment in the campaign.

Two months later, she urged a group of Methodist church leaders to "swing the election" by asking their congregations to vote against Smith. This led the New York governor to charge that Willebrandt was inciting religious bigotry because she was asking a Protestant group to vote against a Roman Catholic. Willebrandt denied the charge, noting that her speech had never mentioned Smith's religion directly, focusing more on his record in regard to Prohibition. Still, the reaction to her speech wounded Willebrandt. "Most of us have a vulnerable spot where we can really be hurt," she wrote of the incident, "and the charge of religious intolerance found mine." On the heels of the Smith controversy, the press began poking into her past. It was at this point that her 1924 divorce became public knowledge.

In June 1929, Willebrandt resigned her position in the Justice Department. Though it was never stated publicly, she had been nudged out by Hoover following his election victory because he felt that her controversial actions reflected badly on his administration. Before leaving the stage, however, Willebrandt wrote a series of articles that were published in serial form in August 1929 and later collected as *The Inside of Prohibition*. She stood by her contention that Prohibition could and should be enforced, but she also spoke openly of the shortcomings that she had observed. She noted the poor quality of Prohibition agents, the harmful meddling of politicians in enforcement efforts, and the lack of support from state governments. She singled out a few people for criticism, including General Lincoln C. Andrews, who had served as assistant secretary of treasury in charge of Prohibition. More than anything else, Willebrandt argued that Prohibition enforcement should be centralized under the direction of one person in the Justice Department. Her recommendations were never acted on.

Willebrandt resumed her private practice after leaving the Justice Department. One of her first clients was Fruit Industries, Inc., a marketing cooperative formed by grape growers. Among their products were packages of grape concentrate that could be used to make wine at home. Many people criticized Willebrandt for going from dry enforcer to wet wine pusher. The complaints grew louder when Willebrandt helped Fruit Industries secure a loan of $1 million from the Federal Farm Board.

Willebrandt continued to practice law until the early 1960s, eventually returning to Southern California. Among her clients was the Screen Directors' Guild, which embroiled her in some of the anti-Communist Hollywood debates of the 1950s. She also devoted a lot of time to raising her adopted daughter, Dorothy. Willebrandt began to suffer poor health in the early 1960s. She died of lung cancer on April 6, 1963, at her home in Riverside, California.

Sources

Brown, Dorothy M. *Mabel Walker Willebrandt: A Study of Power, Loyalty, and Law*. Knoxville, TN: University of Tennessee Press, 1984.

Coffey, Thomas M. *The Long Thirst: Prohibition in America, 1920-1933*. New York: Norton, 1975.

Willebrandt, Mabel Walker. *The Inside of Prohibition*. Indianapolis, IN: The Bobbs-Merrill Company, 1929.

PRIMARY SOURCES

Purley A. Baker of the Anti-Saloon League Calls for National Prohibition

In the Anti-Saloon Yearbook 1914, *the Anti-Saloon League's General Superin- Baker proclaimed the organization's support for a constitutional amendment and the sale of alcohol.*

THE NEXT AND FINAL STEP.

The policy of the anti-Saloon League since its inception has been to go just as fast and just as far as public sentiment would justify. It confines its efforts to law enforcement and sentiment building where that is the only poli- cy public sentiment will sustain. It is for local Prohibition where that policy meets the requirements of the most advanced public demand. It always has favored the adoption of state and national Prohibition just as quickly as an enlightened public conscience warrants. We believe the time is fully ripe for the launching of a campaign for national Prohibition—not by any party or parties, but by the people. That does not mean that we are to relax our efforts one iota for law enforcement, local Prohibition and Prohibition by states, but it is a recognition of the fact that the task begun more than a hundred years ago should speedily be completed.

THE CHARACTER OF THE TRAFFIC.

Every defense the liquor traffic has erected has been battered down except the defenseless appeal to greed and appetite. It no longer has advo- cates: it must depend for its existence upon partisans. It is united with the white slave traffic. The offspring of this unholy union are robbery, bribery, cruelty, debauchery and murder. The martyred Senator Carmack but uttered an accepted truth when he said, "The liquor traffic would rather die than obey the law." It is an enemy to everything that is good in private and public life. It is the friend of everything that is bad. In the name of decent civil gov- ernment and for the sake of humankind the manufacture and sale of this despoiler of the race should be abolished.

THE PERIL WE FACE.

The vices of the cities have been the undoing of past empires and civi- lizations. It has been at the point where the urban population outnumbers the rural people that wrecked Republics have gone down. There the vices have centered and eaten out the heart of the patriotism of the people, making them easy victims of every enemy. The peril of this Republic likewise is now clearly seen to be in her cities. There is no greater menace to democratic institutions than the great segregation of an element which gathers its ideas of patriotism and citizenship from the low grogshop and which has proved its enmity to organized civil government. Already some of our cities are well nigh submerged with this unpatriotic element, which is manipulated by the still baser element engaged in the un-American drink traffic and by the kind of politician the saloon creates. The saloon stands for the worst in political life. All who stand for the best must be aggressively against it. If our Republic is to be saved the liquor traffic must be destroyed.

WHAT HAS BEEN ACCOMPLISHED.

More than half the counties of the Republic, multitudes of the incorporated villages and cities, and nine entire States containing upward of forty-six million people—50 per cent of the population—embracing above two-thirds of the entire territorial area of the country, have outlawed the saloon. The traffic has been driven from the army and navy, from immigrant stations and from the National Capitol; but the greatest triumph of the temperance forces of the nation was the passage of the Webb-Kenyon bill over President Taft's veto, not only for the service it will render the cause of law enforcement, but for the demonstrated fact that Congress is responsive to the organized, expressed will of the people on this as on other important moral issues.

NATIONAL PROHIBITION—HOW SECURED.

National Prohibition can be secured through the adoption of a constitutional amendment by Congress and ratification of the same by the necessary three-fourths—thirty-six—States. A State once having ratified the amendment cannot rescind its action, but a state failing in its effort to ratify may do so at any future time.

THE OPPORTUNE TIME.

The time for nation-wide movement to outlaw the drink traffic is auspicious. Organization is now established and in operation in all parts of the country. The forces that definitely oppose the traffic are in accord as at no time in the past. The moral, scientific and commercial aspects of the problem

148

are being more intelligently put before the public than hitherto. The narrow, acrimonious and emotional appeal is giving way to a rational, determined conviction that the traffic being the source of so much evil and economic waste and the enemy of so much good has no rightful place in our modern civilization.

Abraham Lincoln reluctantly consented to the levying of an Internal Revenue tax as a war measure only when assured by members of his cabinet and leaders in Congress that it would be repealed at the close of the war. When the war was ended and the broken fortunes of the Republic were manifest, the liquor traffic, with that serpent-like wisdom for which it is noted, was the first to urge the continuation of this tax, knowing the force of the bribe upon the public conscience. From that time to the present the chief cry against national Prohibition has been that the government must have the revenue. The adoption of the income tax amendment to the federal constitution furnishes an answer to the revenue problem.

We appeal to every church, to all organized philanthropies and to every individual, of every race and color, who loves his country and his kind, to join in this crusade for a saloonless nation. We depend for success upon the same Leader who commanded Moses to "speak to the children of Israel that they go forward."

P. A. Baker
General Superintendent Anti-Saloon League of America.

Source: *Anti-Saloon Yearbook 1914*. Compiled and edited by Ernest Hurst Cherrington. Westerville, Ohio: The Anti-Saloon League of America, 1914.

The Eighteenth Amendment

This amendment became part of the United States Constitution on January 16, 1919. Prohibition began one year later, on January 17, 1920.

Section 1. After one year from the ratification of this article the manufacture, sale, or transportation of intoxicating liquors within, the importation thereof into, or the exportation thereof from the United States and all territory subject to the jurisdiction thereof for beverage purposes is hereby prohibited.

Section 2. The Congress and the several states shall have concurrent power to enforce this article by appropriate legislation.

Section 3. This article shall be inoperative unless it shall have been ratified as an amendment to Constitution by the legislatures of the several states, as provided in the Constitution, within seven years from the date of the submission hereof to the states by the Congress.

Source: U.S. Constitution, Amendment 18. http://www.archives.gov/national_archives_experience/charters/constitution_amendments_11-27.html

Primary Sources: Charlie Burns Recalls Running a Speakeasy

Charlie Burns Recalls Running a Speakeasy

In the following excerpt from John Kobler's Ardent Spirits, *Charlie Burns recounts his experiences as a co-owner of illegal drinking establishments in New York City during Prohibition (material that appears in brackets is in the original text).*

In 1919, when I was eighteen, I went to the New York University School of Commerce to study accounting. Jack Kriendler was a distant cousin—our families had immigrated from Austria and we lived near each other on the Lower East Side—and he attended Fordham.... The year I graduated, 1922, Jack and a classmate named Eddie Irving bought a controlling interest in a type of place near the campus known as a "Village [*Greenwich Village*] tea room." They called it the Redhead. In addition to food they sold liquor in one-ounce flasks, miniatures, which the customer could drink right there if they wished or take home. They asked me to keep the books. They couldn't afford to pay me a salary. So they made me a partner. Our only idea behind the enterprise at the start was to earn enough money to continue our education, I having decided to practice law instead of accountancy and Jack to become a pharmacist. The way things developed, neither of us realized his ambition.

The Redhead served good, solid, simple food—Jack had a natural culinary gift—and the best liquor we could find. We dealt with two neighborhood bootleggers who would deliver the merchandise to Jack's home on East Fourth Street. When we needed fresh supplies, Jack's kid brothers, Mac and Pete, would wheel it over, a few bottles at a time. Who was going to suspect a couple of kids that age? We never did discover the original source of our liquor, but it was always authentic, imported stuff.

We attracted a small but choice crowd, young people mostly from the schools and colleges, and an occasional tourist. We were a success. But even before we started, we had been approached by a group of Village gangsters who declared themselves in. Being innocent college boys, we refused to discuss the matter. A couple of weeks later they came around again. They told us unless we paid for certain protective services, they would wreck the joint. We remained unimpressed. A few nights later, as Jack and I were walking home, a couple of them jumped us. We gave a pretty good account of ourselves, and they took a pretty good licking. The next time I wasn't so lucky. Jack survived in one piece; but my attacker had a razor, and I wound up in St. Vincent's Hospital with a dozen stitches in my throat. A third fight took place a month later, but again we managed to drive them off.

Meanwhile, we had become acquainted with the district police captain through friends in the James Heron Association. This was a very powerful Lower East Side Democratic organization. These friends let the captain know that Jack and Charlie were decent people who ran an orderly place, no book-making, no gambling, no hookers. He came to see us. "Why didn't you let me know about these things that have been happening to you?" he asked. Jack said: "We didn't understand how serious it was." "I'll see what we can do," he said. And nobody ever bothered us again the whole time we operated in the Village.

Every speakeasy had to make some arrangements with the cops to survive. In our case it wasn't exactly a shakedown, nothing on a regular basis, more like an act of friendship. We would slip the captain a $50 bill from time to time and a box of cigars to the cops on the beat. They could always count on us for free meals and drinks, and at Christmastime, of course, we had a gift for everybody.

In 1925 we sold the Redhead (we had bought out Eddie Irving meanwhile) and opened a place we called the Fronton at 88 Washington Place, a basement nightclub this time with dancing and entertainment. Our star attraction was Al Segal, a great jazz pianist, who later coached performers like Ethel Merman. At the Redhead the door was always open. People just wandered in, paid a 50-cent cover charge on weekend nights and drank their miniature flasks. But the Fronton was a bigger, riskier operation. We felt we had to know our customers. So we kept the front door locked and looked people over carefully through the peephole before we admitted them.

The Fronton prospered, too, and it wasn't long before we heard from our gangster friends again. But we got an unusual break, thanks to a boyhood chum of mine. His name was Jimmy Kerrigan. His father once ran a saloon on Fiftieth Street and Broadway before the Capitol Theater was built there. I peddled newspapers in the area at the age of thirteen, and that's how my path crossed Jimmy's. Well, Jimmy grew up to be a revenue agent, which may explain why we never had any trouble with the feds back at the Redhead.

The minute I got word from those hoodlums that they were planning to visit us on a certain night, I got in touch with Jimmy. He arrived in a car with five of his fellow agents, parked across the street and waited. When the gangsters showed, the agents swarmed all over them. They held a long conversation out there on the sidewalk, and that's the last we ever heard from that particular group.

First a flood, then a flash fire hit the Fronton, and it taught us the importance of having friends in the fire department, as well as the police. Chief Purdy headed the fire brigade nearest us. Off duty he liked to drop in for a few snorts with the missus, and we never charged him anything. One spring day it rained so hard the sewers backed up. Our main room being below street level, the water started rushing up through the toilet bowls and flooding the place. Chief Purdy answered our distress call with powerful pumps and pumped us dry.

Not long after, the flash fire broke out. We never found out how it started. This time Chief Purdy and his men arrived with axes and started to wreck the premises. "Think of all the money you're going to get from the insurance," he said. "My God!" I told him. "We're not insured!" He felt terrible. "Never mind," he said, "we'll fix it all up." And they did, too.

The construction of the Sixth Avenue subway forced us to abandon the Fronton in 1926, and we moved uptown into a brownstone house with an iron gate at 42 West Forty-ninth Street. The main reason we chose it was that the Italian bootlegger who owned it and wasn't doing too well because he couldn't speak English agreed to guarantee our mortgage payments if we would buy all our stock from him. We found both him and his liquor reliable. In fact, if we overbought, he would always take back a few cases. We quickly established a reputation for our French and Italian cooking and our cellar.

Soon after we opened, a police captain from the Forty-seventh Street station came to pay his respects and explain that to protect himself, he had to make a friendly arrest—that is, to put it on the record that we sold liquor. "Now you just leave a couple of pints out in the open," he told us. "We'll have a man come by and pick them up. But don't worry. You'll go free on bail, and that'll be the end of the matter." Which is exactly how it worked out.

A certain group of federal agents presented a more serious problem. They were young men of good families, socialites, who saw a means of making some extra easy money by joining the Prohibition Unit. To put it crudely, they were shakedown artists. The way we handled them, a number of us speakeasy operators in the neighborhood created a sort of informal association. John Perona of the Bath Club, who later founded El Morocco, was the main negotiator who spoke for us all. When one of those agents tried to make a case against us, we'd tell him: "You know John Perona. Call him. He'll tell you we're all right and he'll take care of everything." Then we'd square it with John. It cost us about a thousand a year, not including free meals and drinks.

Our Forty-ninth Street place changed its name every year in order to avoid continuity in the IRS records-—the Iron Gate, the Grotto, 42, Jack & Charlie's, the Puncheon Club. One evening a Yale student named Ben Quinn came in, took a quick look around and cried: "My God, this is my old home! I grew up here!" He was right. The house had passed through several hands since his father sold it. Ben became a regular visitor, and the place was sometimes called "Ben Quinn's kitchen."

In spite of all the payoffs we did have one serious raid. It was ordered personally by Mabel Walker Willebrandt. Two things put her on our trail. First, the rumor that we were the only New York speakeasy in continuous operation that had never been bothered by city police or the feds. Secondly, a valued customer, a Southern gentleman, who didn't trust his local brew, telephoned to ask us to send him some of our whiskey. The employee who took the call stupidly sent it through the mail with the return address on the package. The post office spotted it, reported it to the prohibition authorities and made Mrs. Willebrandt doubly determined to get us, selling liquor through the mail being an additional offense.

It was a long-drawn-out case, but thanks to our able counselor-at-law we reached a compromise. We pleaded guilty to possession of liquor and paid a fine. Ironically, the raid turned out to be the best advertising we ever got. It made us. Because the confiscated liquor was analyzed by federal chemists, who declared it to be of the finest quality. The press cheered. H. L. Mencken wrote, as nearly as I can remember: "Why raid a place that is serving good liquor and not poisoning anybody?"

Although we owned the building on Forty-ninth Street, we only leased the ground, and in 1929 the lease ran out. By then the Rockefellers, who had bought up or leased a lot of land in the Forties and Fifties, including our location, were planning to construct Rockefeller Center. So we had to move again. We didn't want to leave the neighborhood, not after the good relations we had established there with various prohibition agents. We considered several houses in West Fifty-third and West Fifty-fourth, but there were Rockefellers living on both those streets, and they didn't like speakeasies. Nobody exactly liked to have a speakeasy as a neighbor, but some people were more broad-minded than others. We finally settled for the brownstone we've occupied ever since at 21 West Fifty-second.

The last night on Forty-ninth Street, which was not that long before a wrecking crew started to tear down the building, we threw a private farewell party for some of our favorite customers. Bea Lillie, for example. And Bob Benchley. We gave every guest a crowbar or spade and let them go to work breaking down the walls and digging up the floor. Then we all loaded the bottles, crockery, furnishings and so forth onto carts and wheeled them three blocks to our new address.

We weren't there very long before three hoodlums paid us a visit. They represented Jack "Legs" Diamond. [*Of all the gang overlords, possibly the most barbarous. The nickname derived from his fleet-footedness as an adolescent thief. It amused him, a kidnapper, as well as bootlegger, hijacker, extortioner and dope dealer, to burn the bare soles of his captives' feet with matches. He killed, or ordered to be killed, dozens of competitors. He himself was shot up so often that the underworld dubbed him the "Clay Pigeon."*] It was like the old days in the Village again. Diamond wanted a piece of our business. The doorman threw the hoodlums out. We were lucky. Before Diamond had a chance to strike back at us, he was shot to death.

We continued on friendly terms with the prohibition agents. We also became quite friendly with some of the assistant U.S. attorneys, who would drop in for an occasional drink or when they needed a good bottle as a gift would ask us to help them out. But you could never be sure. You could never relax completely. Some new officials might be appointed to the New York district or the agents you took care of might be reassigned elsewhere, and the first thing you knew you got raided.

We had this engineer we trusted, and he installed a series of contraptions for us that worked on different mechanical or electrical impulses. For example, the shelves behind the bar rested on tongue blocks. In case of a raid the bartender could press a button that released the blocks, letting the shelves fall backward and dropping the bottles down a chute. As they fell, they hit against angle irons projecting from the sides of the chute and smashed. At the bottom were rocks and a pile of sand through which the liquor seeped, leaving not a drop of evidence. In addition, when the button was pressed, an alarm bell went off, warning everybody to drink up fast. We once put too many bottles on the shelves and they collapsed under the weight. Another time a bartender pressed the button by mistake. But we had only one serious raid. The agents searched the building for twenty-four hours. They never found a single contraption.

The most important was the secret door to our wine cellar. *[Here Burns led the author down to the subterranean depths of the building. We paused before an alcove, its white walls bare, and he produced a long, thin steel rod.]* Unless you know where to look, all you can see are solid walls, no visible cracks of any kind. But there's this tiny aperture here. You'd have to have an eagle eye. *[He shoved the rod through.]* When I push this a little further in, you'll hear a noise. That's the tongue lock being released on the other side. It takes very little pressure on my part, even though with the steel frame support the thing weighs over a ton. It works like a trigger on a gun. Listen. *[I heard a sharp, metallic click, and the wall swung back on silent hinges, revealing bin upon bin of bottles cradled on their sides.]* This is the only entrance or exit. No other way in or out. If the mechanism broke, we'd have to dig through the concrete and pull out the whole lock. But that never happened. And no agent ever discovered the cache either. We still keep the contraption because people like to come down here and see the way things were in the old days.

Source: Kobler, John. *Ardent Spirits: The Rise and Fall of Prohibition*. New York: G. P. Putnam's Sons, 1973.

Bill McCoy Remembers Rum Row

After retiring from the rumrunning business, famed rumrunner Bill McCoy recalled his Prohibi-
tion-era exploits to journalist Frederick F. Van de Water, who put them together in a first-person
account called The Real McCoy. *In the following passage from* The Real McCoy, *Bill McCoy*
explains how his rum-running ship, the Arethusa, *conducted its trade in illegal alcohol.*

Whenever there was the slimmest chance of making the trip successfully, sea skiffs came out from the Jersey shore to my schooner. I was
selling my rye for $60 a case. On the beach it was gobbled up eagerly
at $120—profit that made these fishermen willing to take all sorts of risks.

They would come wabbling and bouncing out in their little open craft,
one man steering, the other pumping for dear life, and swing in under my
schooner's lee. Usually it was too rough to tie up. Four of us would hold the
skiff away from our side with oars and boat hooks, and we would throw the
"hams" of liquor out to her crew.

The buyer would toss a roll of bills to me. "Twelve thousand dollars for
200 cases, Bill," he would shout. There was no time to count it then. I would
stow it away in my desk drawer and leave my dog on watch. When the customers had gone I would check up. Apart from the one man who had tried
to pass counterfeit $20 bills, no one who traded with my schooner ever
attempted to cheat me. I don't believe any so-called legitimate business can
equal that record.

My sales were made in the midst of confusion and haste, often after
nightfall, and to men I had never seen before and might never encounter
again. It would have been easy to cheat me, since it was known that I did not
count the cash I received until later. There was no possibility of reprisal if I
did discover fraud. Yet at the end of a sojourn on the Row, when I totaled the
proceeds on the way home, the result was always correct, or more than I had
calculated I should have.

The cash, nearly always, was in large denominations, usually $1,000
bills with a sprinkling of $5,000 and $10,000 notes. If a bootlegger handed
you $100 certificates, he apologized, as the average man might if he paid a
debt in pennies. The larger bills I usually slipped between the pages of
Bowditch or my Bible. The rest I stuffed into my desk drawer. I always dread-
ed the task of sorting and counting these yellow and green slips and post-
poned it as long as I could. You may think a job like that would be thrilling

157

and exciting. It wasn't. It was confusing, tedious, down-right hard work. The joys of riches are overestimated if you have to sit down and count them.

Most daring of the sea-skiff men who worked off New Jersey's shore was Geriard Haldenbach, a lad who would ride his little boat through a yelping nor'wester as calmly as a nurse guides a baby-carriage. Frequently we would be hove to, debating whether to stay in the Row or run before the storm, when the lookout would shout:

"Boat coming."

I would know it was Geriard. He drove through weather that kept all other sea-skiff owners ashore, thanking God they were there. With the sea bursting into foam about him, with the planks of his skiff's bottom smacking the waves like giant handclapping, he would come roaring out to buy.

The first day I saw him was one of the dirtiest during which we hung onto the Row. He came under the lee of the *Arethusa* with a foot of water slopping about in the bottom of his skiff and a boy working the pump.

"Fifty cases," Geriard yelled and tossed payment aboard. The rollers were running short and high against the ebb tide and the sea skiff and the schooner were rising and falling as though they were on alternating elevators. I said: "Son, you don't want to try to haul more than twenty-five cases today. If you had any sense, you'd be ashore, anyhow."

"Fifty cases," he repeated. "I know my boat."

We were holding him off with oars and boat hooks. A big wave lifted the *Arethusa*, and as she dropped into its trough the same roller heaved the sea skiff aloft and literally floated it onto our deck. Waist deep in water, we got it clear before the schooner rose again. Geriard only grinned while we cussed him plenty, but we all admired his nerve. He got his fifty cases and made shore. Thereafter he was one of my steady customers when I was on the Row. He told me he was in the game and taking the chances he did because he had just married a girl and wanted her to have the best of everything in the world.

"I make $3,000 a trip," he said. "She's worth taking risks for."

He died a little later with a Coast Guard's bullet through his brisket; died on the sea skiff we had grown to know so well. He was taking his chance, and the Coast Guard was following orders.

And let an ex-rum runner say right here that those men of the [Coast Guard] cutters who made life misery for me were and are fine, square seamen who did a dirty job most of them didn't like, as cleanly as it could be done. Rumors of all sorts floated around the Row about the men of the service. I never believed them, and I never heard of any of them being proved. There are crooks even in the ministry. I have no reason to love Coast Guards, Treasury agents or Department of Justice men. They combined to put me in jail. I do say, however, that no government in the world has gamer, fairer servants than these. Prohibition enforcement agents are something else again.

Coast Guards in small launches frequently would pursue sea skiffs on the way back from the Row. Such a chase was under way one day when Geriard crossed its line and started to pick up one of the cases the fugitive had flung overboard. The pursuer fired at random and shot the lad dead. He had only meant to scare him away.

...

In early 1923 Rum Row was in its heyday. I used to look at that long line of craft, anchored all the way from Montauk to Cape May, with the pride a first settler would feel in the growth of his town.

Schooners and yachts, windjamming square riggers from Scandinavia, tramps from England and Germany, converted tugs and submarine chasers, anything with a bottom that would float and a hold that could be filled with booze, they stretched away in a long line, bowing to the surges, swinging with the tide and wind, waiting in apathy all day for the strenuous activity that began as soon as night fell. Up and down that long line white cutters plodded, surveying the old-timers, inspecting new arrivals. Dories floundered across from ship to ship as the captains and crews of the fleet exchanged visits. It was a roaring, boisterous, sinful-and-glad-of-it, marine Main Street of shifting membership and continually increasing in size, and I was its founder and first citizen.

Beside the rust-streaked iron square riggers and tramps and the black, frowzy schooners of the fleet, my *Arethusa*, with her white hull and slim, well kept lines, stood out like a lovely lady in a slum. She was the most famous and fairest ship on the Row. When we were there we sold out more rapidly than anyone else. She was McCoy's ship, and she carried the real McCoy liquor, genuine, the best procurable, and uncut.

159

My reputation was all the advertisement I needed. Until the [Coast Guard] cutters began to be annoying I sold my liquor almost as fast as we could bring it up from the hold. One night that summer, when the sea was calm and all America apparently wanted a drink, I set the Rum Row record by unloading into small craft 3,400 cases between 5 and 10 P.M. I could have sold twice as much that night if I had had it, but they cleaned us out, and at 10 we sailed back to Nassau for more.

When we reached the Row and anchored, my brother Ben would come out to greet us, bringing fresh meat, vegetables, tobacco, water, newspapers, and magazines. Now that the *Arethusa* had an engine to move her quickly when necessary, we would anchor if it were flat calm and prepare for business. Otherwise we would jog about. Anchor or not, the trade came to us fast enough.

My reputation and the white form of the *Arethusa* riding on the Row were all the advertisement I needed. I had an understanding with my customers that if the schooner were flying the British ensign, it was unsafe to come near her by daylight. If she flew no flag, we were ready for business. For the guidance of shore boats at night, I placed a brilliant electric light well up in my ship's rigging. We were one of the few craft on the Row to have our own [electric] plant. Unshielded, we found this rigging light made our decks bright as day and gave our operations undesired publicity. After one trial I put the bottom of a barrel underneath the lamp. It could be seen, thus at a distance, but the disk of wood kept the deck and immediate vicinity of the *Arethusa* in deep shadow.

Business, as a rule, began at dusk and continued till just before dawn. Until the cutters began to be severe and inquisitive, boats would run out from shore at any hour, their crew would get a bite to eat aboard while we were loading and then would make a leisurely return to the Long Island or Jersey coast. When supervision tightened, all the work was done at night.

At twilight we would get the hatch off the hold, buckle on the guns we never had to use, and prepare for business. My Gloucester captain had left me early this year, and I had made Arey, skipper of the *Young*, sailing master of the *Arethusa*. Arey, as night fell, would climb aloft and, perched on the cross trees, night glasses in hand, watch for cutters or snooping revenue men.

"Boat coming," he would call down. We could see the craft just before it reached us, in the glow of our masthead lamp. Then it would slide into the great circle of shadow shed by the barrel bottom and come alongside. Someone would sing out, "A hundred Black & White" and toss up a roll of bills. Seamen, supervised by Gilletts, my mate, would pass the "hams" over the rail. They would be stowed away in the shore boat, motors would roar, and she would be away, her crew happy in the possession of an extra case for themselves. I always gave the lads presents of whisky, and always a drink, whether they bought from me or not.

At times, when business was brisk, there would be fifteen skiffs, launches, and other varieties of motorboat lying alongside, side by side, at one time, each with its engine pounding until you had to screech to be heard. Wads of bills would be shoved at me from all directions. My pockets would jam so full that I would have to go below several times a night and empty them into my desk where Old Faithful mounted guard. Everyone was eager to get away. Everyone wanted to be loaded at once. The *Arethusa's* deck would be as confused and noisy as the floor of the Stock Exchange on a busy day.

Men whom I knew loaded their own boats. A regular customer would cram his roll into my hands and shout, "A hundred Lawson's, Bill." I would screech back, "Port hold, Jake. Help yourself." No one ever took more liquor than he bought. No one ever short-changed me in paying for it.

After midnight, as a rule, the trade would slacken. By 3 A.M., when the lights went out on the Asbury Park boardwalk, we knew our work was practically over. We would watch a new day come out of the sea, and then would roll into our bunks and sleep, utterly exhausted, far into the morning.

Accommodating customers on shore would send us off a boat with the morning papers and milk. We had all the comforts of home on the Row and some no home would harbor. Cash was so thick there and men so generous that daughters of joy [prostitutes] actually started a navy of their own and embarked on Rum Row, sailing instead of street walking.

We lived high. Besides the food brought out to us from New York—we frequently lay so close to the harbor mouth that on clear days we could see the white spire of the Woolworth Building shining above the shore haze—the mackerel fleet hovered about, more than willing to exchange a mess of fresh-caught fish for a few bottles of liquor. Lobstermen gave us their short lobsters for whisky. Scallop boats dredged back and forth. More often than not these last were semi-bootleggers who trawled industriously when the cutter hung around and bought liquor by the twenty-five cases when they were absent.

Rum Row, incidentally, was the direct means of opening up several new vast scallop beds. While pretending to be fishing during the presence of cutters, the crews found to their surprise that they were trawling scallops where they had never known they grew. The cream of sea food and the best of shore supplies were ours. We lived well and were happy.

Source: Van de Water, Frederic F. *The Real McCoy*. Garden City, N.Y.: Doubleday, Doran & Company, 1931.

Izzy Einstein on His Adventures as a Prohibition Agent

In the following passage from his memoir Prohibition Agent No. 1, *Izzy Einstein recalls his experiences in pursuing violators of the Volstead Act in Rhode Island.*

Only half-pint size and with a coastline that was ideal for rum runners, Rhode Island never took to Prohibition. When the Eighteenth Amendment came up for ratification, this littlest state in the Union turned it down with a bang and a Bronx cheer; and ever since then Rhode Island has been giving the authorities in Washington more worry than Texas and California combined. To bring about any sort of enforcement there was a pip of a problem.

Finally, in September of 1922, it was decided that something drastic would have to be done. I received orders, along with about twenty-five other agents, to proceed to Providence. We were to cooperate with the local forces; and that would have been easy, because the local forces weren't doing anything. In fact, the majority of the local personnel was in the act of getting fired right down to stenographers and charwomen. So that rather left it up to us. And, as I found out, we were being kept tabs on by some special agents from the Intelligence Department in Washington, sent on for the purpose.

Well, we checked in at various hotels in town under the best names we could think of. I put up at the Biltmore. And then we got busy as quietly as possible. We decided that if people in this city and state didn't know what Prohibition meant, we wouldn't give them any hints of it till we had had a chance to gather some evidence. Furthermore, we had been specially cautioned by Washington that in this town bootleggers had an uncanny way of learning about intended raids a couple of days before they happened; for it was not only a wet town but also a very "leaky" one.

So we started in, watching our step at every turn, and the first day everything went serenely. Apparently nobody knew we'd come. But the second day, as we were sauntering around, dropping in here and there for a look, I noticed that things were tightening up a bit. Just something in the air. You could feel it. And so I wasn't entirely surprised when a man came up to me at the hotel and said he'd like to invite me to a little party that evening—a dinner at a social club he belonged to. He introduced a couple of his friends to me and they all said they hoped I'd come. I didn't know just what the idea was, but I knew it was something. So I told them I couldn't give a definite answer at the moment, but would let them know later if I'd be able to accept their invitation.

Good thing I stalled! Hardly an hour afterward, I was tipped off by one of the Intelligence men, who was a personal friend of mine. He told me about the merry little party that had been framed for me. It was to be "quite a surprise"—in the form of much liquor and jazzy dames—and I was to be caught by reporters and flash-light camera men in a way that would fry my goose as a Government agent. How my friend found out I don't know. That was his business, and he was good at it. But on the strength of what he told me I informed by intended hosts that I wasn't feeling well.

Next day, before things got any more tanglefoot for us, I slipped out and, in company with some other agents, went scouting around town in some of the outlying districts—Pawtucket, Woonsocket and so on. It's a great region for textile mills, and mill hands aren't generally millionaires, so we wore old clothes in making our calls at the saloons. And we varied things a bit by being longshoremen part of the time, and then hod-carriers, also coalbearers, fruit peddlers and just plain street corner bums.

A couple of us began the day's work by ordering an early breakfast at a spaghetti establishment I had my suspicions of. We arrived so early that the proprietor hadn't come yet, but the bartender-waiter, who was just opening up, offered us a table and then went back into the kitchen to prepare the food. I chose this opportunity to take a look behind the bar. He heard me, came rushing out and grabbed a revolver from somewhere, telling me to stay perfectly still or he'd plug me. I showed my badge and that changed his mind.

Later, with hods and shovels, we stopped in for rest and refreshment at a saloon run by a man named Woodwick who sold us stuff that was first-cousin to Wood Alcohol. When we flashed our badges and handed him a summons he keeled over, just as though he'd drunk some of his own liquor. We left him in the care of his bartender who had a nice name too: Bourbonnaris. On the summons it looked like a new name for Kentucky Highball.

Most of these places—we "left cards" at about thirty—were wide open. But there was one that had a foxy system: the bartender wearing an overcoat with a different kind of bottle in every pocket. In case of a raid he could walk out with the supply and hide or destroy it, and there'd be nothing found. We managed, however, to nab this stuff while still "on the hoof."

At another saloon one of my companions bummed a drink in exchange for a tip, though at first the bartender was skeptical.

"Tell me your tip," he said, "and we'll see if it's worth a drink."

The tip was that there were Federal agents on the job in the neighborhood. He got the drink. And a few minutes later the recipient of this valuable information was handed a little "tip" with our compliments.

But there was one fellow we were particularly after, and that was a man named Taylor, proprietor of a place in Central Falls, just outside of Providence, in regard to whom the Department had received numerous complaints. This fellow was reputed to have boasted that "no Federal gumshoer could get him." So we had his name, you might say, at the top of our visiting list.

Well, I took a ride in a car past his place to see what it looked like, and I noticed that the street in front was torn up with a new sewer being put in, and that men with picks and shovels were at work in little groups all up and down the block. That gave me an idea. Went back into town and returned with a couple of other agents, the three of us armed with shovels and with old bandannas around our necks, Italian style. We set to work dishing the dirt along with the other shovelers, and the sewer contractor, whoever he was, never guessed that he got about a dollar's worth of shoveling he didn't pay for. Then we took time off to slake our whistles at the establishment of Mr. Taylor.

He welcomed us and our shovels cordially enough, responding to our requests for whiskey by pouring some "amber fluid" (as they say in court) out of a large earthenware pitcher. But when I jumped behind the bar to grab the evidence, he saw me out of the corner of his eye, made a quick turn, and dumped the entire contents of the pitcher in my face. It stung my eyes, almost blinding me for the moment, and my whole shirt was drenched with the stuff.

Maybe I murmured something. (He claimed afterward that I used impolite language on the premises.) I'm not much of a cusser; but then, on the other hand, I'm not used to having stuff like that flung in my eyes and down my bosom—so perhaps an exclamation escaped me. Anyhow he certainly escaped me, dashing out of the place like mad and hoofing it a couple of blocks. Then he hopped on a passing truck and kept going.

We gave chase, and what a chase it turned out to be! I was heavily per-
fumed with "amber liquid," an aroma which any one nearby would have
taken for *Eau de Distillery*, and with perfect reason. With the aid of a car we
commandeered we caught up with the nimble Nurmi [Paavo Nurmi, a famed
Olympic runner of the 1920s], and took him in charge.

"Why did you run?" I asked him.

"You told me you were Izzy Einstein," he said, "and that was enough."

At the Police Station where we brought him the officer at the desk
seemed anything but eager to accept him, even as a gift. I showed my badge,
told who I was, explained that he had sold me liquor, and still the officer
made out he couldn't understand why I was bringing the man in. He treated
my prisoner better than he treated me. But I finally persuaded him to keep
him with instructions that friend Taylor was to appear before the United
States Commissioner in Providence to answer to the following charges: 1.
selling whiskey; 2. possessing whiskey; 3. maintaining a nuisance; 4. interfer-
ing with government officers in the performance of their duty.

There were forty-five others who were due to answer charges, so he had
no occasion to feel lonesome.

Next morning when I went to the Woolworth Building where the United
States commissioner had his headquarters, and where all these people with
summonses were due to report, I found a big crowd waiting outside. Newspaper reporters were bobbing about and camera men were on the trigger in
strategic locations. I could hear clicks as I ran the gauntlet of them to get
inside the building.

"What's all the excitement?" I asked a friend of mine whom I met in the
corridor.

He told me. The news, which I was apparently the last person to learn,
was that Taylor had gotten a firm of attorneys to file a complaint against me
and two other agents; he had filed suit in the Providence County Superior
Court, charging me with "trespass and assault" and seeking $10,000 damages.

"Trespass and assault," was good!

I had walked into a wide-open place of business, reached for a pitcher he
had served me from, and been given a free whiskey bath. If that's "trespass
and assault," then I'm a Chinaman.

Damn clever these Rhode Islanders!

While I am standing there learning this piece of news and trying to make sense of it, a deputy sheriff walks up to me with a warrant.

"Are you Federal Agent Isidor Einstein?" he asks me.

I tell him I am, and he arrests me in the name of the law of the state of Rhode Island. Says he's very sorry to do this, and that he's in sympathy with me, but that he is obliged to carry out the law. I tell him I understand his position, and to go ahead and do his duty. As a result of my taking it that way and not making any fuss, he lets me ride over to the Courthouse in a taxi by myself, on my assurance that I'll go surrender myself at the sheriff's office.

The other two agents who are approached by deputies with warrants don't take it so peaceably. They get mad. One of them refuses even to own up to his name, till I tell him he'd better, and then he takes a sock at the sheriff and has to be literally choked into submission—which is of course swell stuff for the newspaper fellows to play up, but not so good for the Department. Anyhow these agents both of them try to show they are above the state law, and both get dragged off in handcuffs for the trouble they make.

Oddly enough I, the non-resister, was the one that got the headlines—the Boston *American*, for example, announcing on its front page in letters two inches high:

IZZY EINSTEIN, BOOZE RAIDER, ARRESTED

In nearly every paper that sprang the story on its readers—and it went clear down to Georgia—my name was the featured one, even though the account of the scrimmages that occurred didn't list me as an active participant.

Well maybe when a prisoner *doesn't* sock a sheriff, it's news.

Anyhow I taxied peaceably as a Rhode Island clam to the sheriff's office, and there I was shown every courtesy. I had hardly got there when a man by the name of David Korn came asking to meet me; so we were presented to each other, and he proceeded to astonish everybody by pulling out of his pocket $100,000 worth of Pennsylvania Railroad bonds, with the suggestion that possibly it might be a convenience to me to have a wad of them put up as my bail. He made this offer as a local citizen who was interested in my work. And I'll say it was kind of him, especially as he was a total stranger to me.

Meanwhile there was a great to-do in Wet circles over the way Enforcement had been foiled; the wires to Washington were kept busy, and there were statements that the sheriffs who had arrested us were in contempt of court. Not being a lawyer I can't give you all the wherefores and whereases of the thing, but the upshot was, that after the legal lights got through, the cases against us were thrown out.

As to the booze dispensers upon whom I served summonses before getting arrested myself, every man of them was held for court. Ditto my prisoner, Mr. Taylor.

Except for these cases, which took me back to Providence twice as a witness, my efforts in Rhode Island were called off on account of Wet Grounds.

Source: Einstein, Izzy. *Prohibition Agent No. 1*. New York: Frederick A. Stokes, 1932.

Walter Lippmann Discusses Nullifying the Eighteenth Amendment

In this essay from Harper's Monthly Magazine, *Walter Lippmann contends that Prohibition is not enforceable and argues that the Supreme Court should formally nullify the Eighteenth Amendment.*

An eminent dry recently set out to write a book that the wets would read. So he called his book *Prohibition at Its Worst*. Ostensibly this title means to say that even at its worst prohibition today is a great blessing, but actually the purpose of this title is to make unsuspecting and narrow-minded wets buy the book because they think it will furnish horrible examples to confirm their prejudice. The author is Irving Fisher, Professor of Economics at Yale University. Nevertheless, the book itself is well worth a careful reading. It tells how Professor Fisher became a total abstainer. It then explains how he overcame his early scruples against prohibition by law. It proceeds to present statistics which are favorable to prohibition and to challenge certain unfavorable statistics. It is the conclusion, however, which is illuminating, for it is there that Professor Fisher is inevitably brought face to face with the predicament of prohibition.

In essence Professor Fisher's conclusions are as follows: "Present conditions are intolerable and must be corrected." A liberalizing of the Volstead Act is unconstitutional, and the constitution cannot be amended. The only alternatives are "enforcement or nullification." This is the predicament. Professor Fisher escapes from it by faith. He believes that prohibition can be enforced. Now I wonder if Professor Fisher realizes fully where his argument has led him. He has said that the only possible way of correcting "intolerable conditions" arising out of the Volstead Act is to enforce the Volstead Act fully. Here, in other words, is a law which cannot be altered to conform to experience or to change in public opinion. This law is immutable. For all practical purposes this law is beyond human control. However intolerable it may become, the only alternative is to enforce it or to defy it. This nation can choose to declare war and to make peace; it can write tariffs and it can alter tariffs; it can admit immigrants and it can bar immigrants. But in respect to prohibition it has lost its sovereignty. To prohibition in the form prescribed by the Volstead Act it is irretrievably committed.

That is Professor Fisher's argument and, if life were not stronger than logic, it would be unanswerable. It is true for example that the Eighteenth

Amendment cannot be repealed. In order to repeal it there would be required two-thirds of the Senate and two-thirds of the House, and a majority of both houses in 37 states. A repeal could, therefore, be vetoed by 33 Senators, or by 146 Representatives, or by a majority in 13 State Senates. A repeal might pass Congress, it might pass 35 Legislatures, it might pass one house in the remaining 13 Legislatures, and still the Eighteenth Amendment would be intact. As long as prohibition has a majority in one branch of the Legislature in 13 states a repeal of the Eighteenth Amendment is impossible. Repeal would have to be fought for in 96 state legislative bodies and the two houses of Congress. Out of these 98 law-making bodies, 13 in 13 separate states possess an absolute veto.

It is also true that the Volstead Act cannot be liberalized without *nullifying the intent* of this immutable Eighteenth Amendment. There is no doubt that the Amendment was intended to prohibit the lightest beer and the lightest wine no less than gin and absinthe. We, therefore, arrive by irresistible logic at the conclusion that the Volstead Act itself is immutable.

Having reached this point, we must examine Professor Fisher's claim that the Volstead Act should be enforced. The question is: can it be? What do we mean by enforcement? We do not mean the absolute disappearance of all liquor. No law is enforced absolutely. The penal law is broken by murderers and thieves. The tariff law is broken by smugglers. The commercial law is broken by swindlers. The tax laws are broken by tax-dodgers. Is a breach of the Volstead Act in the same category of law breaking? Well, *Harper's Magazine* does not publish articles by murderers, thieves, smugglers, swindlers, and tax-dodgers discussing the policy of the law they break. The opponents of capital punishment do not form associations of murderers. The free traders do not hold banquets attended by smugglers. The Secretary of the Treasury does not make speeches to tax-dodgers. But cabinet officers, senators, congressmen, governors, mayors, judges, chiefs of police, bankers, editors, and other pillars of society are openly convivial with men who make no bones about their defiance of the Volstead Act. Now a law which can be violated openly and without shame by men who are normally law-abiding may fairly be called a law which is not enforced.

Such a law is obviously in a different category from a law which is poorly enforced. The income tax law is, I believe, poorly enforced in the sense that many people liable to pay do not make returns, and that many who make returns cheat the law. But who ever heard of a tax-dodger saying, as Mr. Jerome D. Greene does in the *Atlantic Monthly*, that "disregard of the law" should be openly approved and encouraged by those who oppose in principle the Eighteenth Amendment and the Volstead Act?

It is no answer to say that bootleggers are out to make money and not to vindicate a principle, or that most drinkers have more thirst than they have conviction. All that may be true, and still every movement to enforce prohibition must reckon with the capital fact that in regard to this one law the conscience of the community in the wet centers tolerates and even approves the breaking of the law. The leaders of opinion do not wish to see the law enforced. They are glad to read that it is not being enforced. They take pleasure in contemplating the confusion of [Prohibition Unit director] General [Lincoln C.] Andrews. They would not lift a finger to help him. They would not think of reporting a violation. They would not willingly testify for the government. They will not convict if they are on a jury.

II

It is said that this state of mind exists only in the large cities. Granted. Assume that not more than twenty-five per cent of the population lives in large cities. Where are you then? You are then saying that the city population of the United States is openly defiant of one section of the Constitution of the United States. Assume for the sake of the argument that the farmers of the United States all obey it as much as they obey any ordinary law. It is not true, but assume that it is. Assume too that the inhabitants of villages and small towns are essentially law-abiding prohibitionists. And then face the fact that New York, Chicago, Philadelphia, Boston, Washington, San Francisco, St. Louis, Cincinnati, Detroit, and other great centers of population are wet in practice and wet in principle.

Is that important or is it not? Does it not mean a good deal to say that in a nation overwhelmingly interested in business, the business centers are openly defiant of a part of the fundamental law? Even if it were a fact that by count of heads there are more drys than wets in the United States, still that would not mitigate the fact that in at least fifteen or twenty of the most powerful centers of American civilization the majority is greatly against the observance and enforcement of the prohibition law. The cities may be a minority, but if they are a determined minority it will not be easy to coerce them. When

171

the object is to regulate personal habit and social custom, the majority which matters is the majority of the community concerned. A hundred thousand people living in twenty villages will in the long run find it impossible to coerce fifty thousand people living in one city.

There are no reliable figures by which one can measure the size of the opposition to enforcement, or the degree of enforcement. Professor Fisher cites the increase in Federal convictions from 22,000 in 1922 to 38,000 in 1925. The figures are meaningless. No one knows whether there were more bootleggers to catch in 1925 than in 1922. He notes the increase in total penitentiary sentences from 1552 years in 1922 to 3406 years in 1925. These figures are meaningless unless you know what nobody knows: whether the total number of bootleggers increased or decreased. Professor Fisher, with a recklessness that one hardly expects to find in a professor at Yale, announces that "the saloon has gone." He fails to mention that the speakeasy has come in. He estimates by an unknown method of calculation that the total consumption of alcohol today "is certainly less than 16 percent of pre-prohibition consumption, probably less than 10 per cent, and possibly less than 5 per cent." If this computation were correct, Professor Fisher ought to be very happy. A law which is enforced 90 to 95 per cent is very successfully enforced. But of course Professor Fisher does not believe his own figures, for he declares at the conclusion of his study that "present conditions are intolerable."

Now if we could stop 90 or 95 per cent of all murders, robberies, swindles, and other kinds of crime we should feel highly elated about the administration of the law. Yet Professor Fisher finds it "intolerable" because the Volstead Act has reduced the consumption of alcohol to something like 5 per cent of what it was in the bad old days! The estimate is obviously nonsense; Professor Fisher knows it is nonsense. In making it he has yielded to the great temptation of the uncritical statistician which is to name a figure when there is no census of the facts upon which to base any figure.

The problem cannot be discussed intelligently in terms of figures. The reason is simple. On one side of the equation you have an absolute prohibition of all alcoholic drinks. On the other side you have a thirst for such drinks which cannot be measured. You have sources of supply through the diversion of industrial alcohol, through smuggling, through illicit stills and home brews, which are hidden, and cannot be measured. You have a machinery of enforcement of uncertain honesty and efficiency pitted against an

172

intense consumers' demand, against the bootlegging industry inspired by high profits, against the ingenuity of the householders who can manufacture unlimited quantities of poor but thoroughly alcoholic concoctions in their own cellars and kitchens. The attempt to measure these elements is a statistical absurdity, for they are all variable and none can be counted. You might as well produce statistics on the number of daily conversations in the United States on the subject of the weather.

III

The real problem of prohibition enforcement turns on the intensity of the conviction in certain communities not merely that the law is a failure, but that it ought to be a failure. The ultimate obstacle to enforcement is the will of an important body of American citizens that they will not submit to federal prohibition. They do not recognize the right of the federal government in the premises. They regard the Eighteenth Amendment as obnoxious to the genius of the rest of the Constitution. And they would regard the successful enforcement of the Eighteenth Amendment as a destruction of some part of the soundest American tradition. That is the fact on which at last the whole question of enforcement is posed. There is a conflict between the will of the drys and the will of the wets; and when you look for the "facts" about prohibition you have to remember that they are not inert like a pile of bricks, but that the facts are created from day to day by human wills inspired by appetite, by self-interest, and by high conviction. That is why an increase in the intensity of enforcement will arouse an increase in the intensity of the opposition; why a victory for enforcement on one sector means merely the outbreak of violation on another.

It is an optimistic dry who thinks this conflict will subside and that the wets will grow weary of opposition. It is much more probable that the drys will grow weary of enforcement. After all, your teetotaler in Kansas can continue to abstain whether the law is enforced or not. The failure of enforcement does not interfere with his life. But the wet in Chicago has a personal desire to continue breaking the law. The teetotaler has to whip himself up to the effort of caring deeply what the wet in Chicago drinks at his meals. The wet pursues his own desires. The dry, in short, has to be vigilantly unselfish, if that is the proper name for it, but the wet has only to be lazily selfish. The forces of inertia are all on the side of the wets. In the long run ordinary human self-indulgence will, I think, prove stronger than a rather abstract determination to correct it.

Certainly at the end of six years of prohibition the opposition is more intense. There may be less alcohol consumed. One man's guess here is as good as the next man's. But that the wets are politically ever so much stronger than they were when the Amendment was ratified on January 16, 1919, no one can for a moment doubt. East of the Mississippi and north of the Ohio there are few States in which prohibition is not an issue. The Democratic Party in practically every State in that section is now a wet party. These States cast something like two hundred electoral votes. The Republican Party in this same section is either wet or hesitant or worried. There is no doubt that if the Amendment came up for ratification today it could not possibly pass. I have already said I do not think the Amendment can be repealed. I am now saying that it could not again be ratified. All this opposition adds immensely to the difficulty of enforcement. Politicians may say they are all for enforcement while the Amendment is in the Constitution. That is a glib formula. But in fact the stronger the opposition becomes politically, the weaker the enforcement machinery becomes. Local officials will not work so hard to enforce. Congress will hesitate to give the government new powers. Politicians will take good care not to make themselves unpopular by too much activity. That is the way popular government works. If a community is hostile to enforcement, the police look the other way, citizens will not supply evidence, juries will not convict, prosecutors will watch their step, judges will lean over backward in protecting the defendant's rights.

For all these reasons I say it is a fair assumption that we are faced with a law which cannot be enforced and which cannot be repealed. It is a curious dilemma created in part by a defect in the Constitution and in part by a lack of popular wisdom in dealing with the Constitution. By the test of common sense, by the test of popular sovereignty, this nation having decided to try the revolutionary experiment of prohibition ought to be able to modify the law whenever experience shows that it needs to be modified. But the American Constitution is so constructed that it is virtually impossible to delete anything that is once in it. Theoretically, of course, it is just as easy to repeal an amendment as it is to pass it. But our history shows that in fact the veto of the minority is always strong enough to prevent repeal.

Because the Constitution is so difficult to change, it ought obviously never to contain any definite rule of human morality. It ought to remain purely and simply a charter defining the powers of government. Had the Eighteenth Amendment given Congress the power to prohibit liquor, instead of announcing that liquor was prohibited, the whole problem could be handled intelligently, and we should not be facing, as I believe we are, the necessity first of disobeying the Constitution and then of inventing a legal fiction to regularize our disobedience.

IV

However, the fat is in the fire. The Eighteenth Amendment is unrepealable and the human resentment against it unrepealable. Once again, as they have several times in the past, a considerable part of the American people find themselves in a constitutional straitjacket out of which they will have somehow to wriggle free. This business of wriggling free is sometimes called nullification. Technically, nullification is practiced when a state makes it a crime to enforce a particular federal law. Technically, therefore, the rebellion against the Eighteenth Amendment is not nullification.

But that the object of the movement against the Eighteenth Amendment is to nullify the intent of the authors of the Amendment, no candid man can deny. They meant to prohibit all intoxicating liquors throughout the United States. It is the intention of the wets to legalize some or all intoxicating liquors in those states where a majority desires it. That is the objective. The method may be a gradual failure to enforce the law in wet territory, and the reduction of the Eighteenth Amendment to the status of some of the old unrepealed Blue Sunday legislation. The method may be an amendment to the Volstead Act permitting each state to define intoxicating liquor. Many methods are likely to be employed. Their purpose is to change the practical effect of the Eighteenth Amendment even though its language remains the same.

Only those who have read American history through rose-colored glasses will be shocked at this prospect. This is a normal and traditional American method of circumventing the inflexibility of the Constitution. When the Constitution has come into conflict with the living needs of the nation, and when amendment was impossible, the method of changing the Constitution has been to change it and then get the very human Supreme Court to sanction it. The Constitution gives the Presidential electors the right to use their discretion in the choice of a President. They have lost that right. Yet the Constitution has never been amended to take away that right. The Constitution says that no man shall be Senator who is not thirty years old. Henry Clay entered the Senate at twenty-nine; Robert M. LaFollette, Jr., was younger than thirty when he was elected. The Constitution says that Representatives shall be apportioned according to population as determined by a census every ten years. There has been no new apportionment for sixteen years. The provision that slaves should be delivered up on demand was consistently nullified by many Northern States. The provision that the President shall make treaties only with the advice and consent of the Senate was disregarded in important instances both by Roosevelt and Wilson. The Fourteenth Amendment in so far as it provides a penalty for denial of the right to vote is dead. The Fifteenth Amendment is nullified in most if not all the Southern States. If then the Eighteenth Amendment is somehow nullified in certain Northern States, there will be nothing novel or revolutionary about it.

I had some correspondence recently with a public man who was saying that the wet states, and New York in particular, were committing a crime by trying to nullify the Eighteenth Amendment. As he had just made a speech in Georgia on this subject I called his attention to the Fourteenth and Fifteenth Amendments. He replied that after extended study of the election laws of the South he had come to the conclusion that they are not in conflict with the Fifteenth Amendment. That is true. The South now has a set of election laws which have not been declared unconstitutional. Yet under those laws as they are administered, the Southern Negro is effectively disfranchised. The intent of the Fifteenth Amendment was to enfranchise the Negro.

The moral is plain. If liquor is legalized in the States which desire it, all that is necessary to make it constitutional is for the Supreme Court, bowing to public opinion, to find by the proper reasoning that the States are not violating the Eighteenth Amendment. Then they will not be violating it. They will be violating what the authors of it meant. But the Constitution, thank heavens, means whatever a living Supreme Court says it means. And the Supreme Court, thank heavens, is composed on the whole not of worshippers of a sacred text, but of jurists and statesmen and human beings.

No doubt all this will sound irreverent and disorderly to any man who thinks that a people is law-abiding when it obeys the literal injunction of its statutes and lawless when it disobeys them. The matter is not so simple. The history of law shows that it is beyond the wit of man to frame laws which are always clear and simple to follow. That is why so great a part of the evolution of law has come about not through the repeal and amendment of statutes but through judicial, through administrative, and through popular interpretation.

Who can doubt, for example, that the Sherman Anti-Trust Law as interpreted by the courts, and as interpreted by the Attorney-General today is a very different law from that which Congress passed a generation ago? The real law lies not in the words of the law but in the action of the courts and executives. If the test of loyalty to the laws were loyalty to the original intent of each law, we should have to confess that we are a thoroughly lawless people. It is now, and always has been, impossible to obey literally the original intent of all the legal texts.

A community has not ceased to be essentially law-abiding merely because it refuses to practice literal obedience. There is such a thing as orderly disobedience to a statute, a disobedience which is open, frankly avowed, and in conformity with the general sense of what is reasonable. The opponents of the Volstead Act include, of course, bootleggers for profit and drinkers who want to drink. But they include also men and women of high conviction who regard federal prohibition as contrary to the genius of our constitutional system, who think of it as constitutionally immoral. It may seem as if they were in alliance with the bootleggers, but in fact the success of their campaign would be fatal to the bootlegging industry. If they were merely the agents of the bootleggers they would not be seeking, as they are seeking, a revision of the law which would put the bootleggers out of business.

The situation in which we find ourselves is due to a peculiar defect in our constitutional system which stops us from amending the prohibition law. That avenue of reform is closed. We are forced once more, as we have been several times in the past, to assert by disobedience, by agitation, finally by interpretation and acquiescence, the superior rights of experience over a legal text.

Source: Lippmann, Walter. "Our Predicament under the Eighteenth Amendment." *Harper's Monthly Magazine* 154 (December 1926).

Chicago Daily Tribune Reports on the Valentine's Day Massacre

On Friday, February 15, 1929, the Chicago Daily Tribune *published the following story on the alcohol-related murders that would become known as the Valentine's Day Massacre.*

Officials Probe Booze Deals in Gang Shooting

Inquest Today in Seven Deaths

In the state's attorney's investigation last night of the "north side massacre" in which seven men were shot dead against a wall in a garage at 2122 North Clark Street yesterday morning a dovetailing of underworld rumors developed a double motive.

It is the police belief that the gangsters who were killed paid the penalty for being followers of George Moran, successor to Dean O'Banion. The historic antagonist, as history goes in the swift careers of gangsters, of the O'Banion-Moran crew, is Alphonse Capone, otherwise Al Brown.

See 20ᵗʰ Ward Motive

While that historic antagonism furnished the police a background of hate, jealousy, and revenge, it was also reported that a more immediate reason for the seven murders lies in a campaign of Moran's alcohol sellers to take liquor from Detroit sources and with it penetrate the Bloody Twentieth ward, the booze territory of the Capone gang.

While the police under Commissioner Russell and State's Attorney Swanson were hunting evidence a special coroner's jury was impanelled by Coroner Bundesen to investigate the murders of the men listed and described as follows:

Dr. Reinhardt H. Schwimmer, resident of the Parkway hotel, an optometrist with offices in the Capitol building. Had no criminal record, but was known as the companion of hoodlums and was said to have boasted recently that he was in the alky racket and could have any one "taken for a ride."

Peter Gusenberg, 434 Roscoe street, for 27 years a criminal and one of the leaders of the Moran gang.

Albert R. Weinshank, owner of the Alcazar club, 4207 Broadway and an official of the Central Cleaners and Dyers company 2705 Fullerton avenue.

Adam Heyer, alias Frank Snyder, alias Hayes, 2024 Farragut avenue, owner of the S. M. C. Cartage company where the murders took place.

John May, 1249 West Madison street, father of seven children and an ex-safe blower.

James Clark, brother-in-law of Bugs Moran, and said to have a reputation as a hardened killer.

Frank Gusenberg, brother of Peter, who died in the Alexian Brothers' hospital after refusing for an hour to give any information to the police about his assailants.....

As a start in the investigation the state's attorney's office raided Cicero last night, sending in fifteen prisoners, taking them from the Capone strongholds.

Report Moran in Hiding

As officials viewed the bodies after the shooting they sought to locate Moran without success. But last night it was reported by friends of the gang chief that he was secluded and refused even to leave his room. Capone was found to be in Florida superintending his dog track venture there....

Planned Trip to Detroit

"How could this have happened?" detectives who knew the valor of six of the dead men wondered. The explanation came:

"Two of the executioners were in police uniform and the seven men thought they were facing only arrest, yielding to disarming and obeying orders to stand in a row facing the wall. A clever trick. Otherwise the seven men would have sold their lives dearly.

"Were they 'put on the spot'?" the police wondered, thinking it strange that the seven men should have been caught unawares in one of their beer depots at 10:30 a.m. The answer came in a statement that a rum running expedition was contemplated; the Gusenbergs and their aids were to leave for Detroit at noon with several of the trucks then in the garage and they had expected to come back heavily laden with forbidden beverages.

Six of the bodies had been quickly identified during the afternoon, all of them being made positive by a comparison of their finger prints with others on file at the bureau of identification. It was not until late in the evening that it was learned that Dr. Schwimmer was one of the dead.

Dr. Karl Meyer, chief surgeon of the county hospital, recognized Dr. Schwimmers' body. Schwimmer, who called himself a doctor of optometry, had attended a patient Dr. Meyer knew as Peter Gorman—in reality Peter Gusenberg, who was operated on for appendicitis.

Friend of Gang Leaders

Other inquiries brought the word that Schwimmer had been proud to call himself friend of O'Banion and had followed up that association with Hymie Weiss until Weiss was killed, with Vincent Drucci, until Drucci was killed, with the Gusenbergs until they were killed and with them, the doctor.

Dr. Schwimmer was divorced in 1923 from his wife, Fae Johnson Schwimmer, and then he went to live at the Parkway hotel, where O'Banion and his gang lived under assumed names and under assumed respectability. He was requested to leave there because of his debts and hotel attaches recalled that he returned there some time later, announcing that he had married a Mrs. Risch, a wealthy widow, and that henceforth he would quit associating with hoodlums.

But the former Mrs. Risch divorced him a year or so ago, the detectives were told, and Schwimmer returned to his old ways, telling his acquaintances he enjoyed sharing in the dangers of the Moran gang in bringing in contraband here from Detroit. Recently he talked of sharing in the profits, those who knew him told the authorities, and he told of what a power he was on the north side, fearing no one and able to have whoever he willed put to death.

The information available about Weinshank caused the officials to pause and consider the feud between cleaning and dyeing associations as a possible reason for the slaughter of yesterday. Weinshank had become some kind of a power in the Central Cleaning and Dyeing company, 2705 Fullerton avenue, manager or business agent of the employees' union, the detectives did not establish which.

That is an organization of many small shop keepers who send garments to the central establishment, which is a cooperative venture, for cleaning, and which had considerable trouble, having its garments explode, its trucks wrecked and its employees slugged and intimidated. Racketeers were seeking to take over the entire industry in Chicago and the Becker system, for protection, gave an interest in its business to Alphonse Capone.

The Central association thereupon engaged the services of the Moran gang, Moran, Pete Gusenberg and Willie Marks being given some sort of a financial guarantee. As this gang was already deeply involved with a rum feud with the Capone gang, the business rivalry intensified the hatreds of the rival gangs.

Booze Basis of It All

But before much consideration had been given to that phase of the gang war, the officials came to the conclusion that but one thing could have engendered sufficient venom for seven murders—booze. As United States District Attorney George E. Q. Johnson put it:

"This ghastly occurrence is further proof of a statement I have made a number of times. From reports it appears that this murderous mob was engaged in the violation of the national prohibition act."

Still another possibility cropped up, however. Some police recalled that Frank Miller had been released from the penitentiary recently after serving a sentence for his part in the $1,000,000 Werner Brothers Warehouse safe-blowing of several years ago. Miller let some of his friends know that he felt he had been illy treated by O'Banion and Moran, who were said by him to have suggested the looting of the safety deposit boxes of the warehouse.

Mention McGurn Attack

Again, it was said that the Gusenbergs were responsible for the attempt on the life of Jack McGurn at the McCormick hotel a year ago and that McGurn was a free lance gunman who always paid his gun debts.

But, harking back to the gang killings of the last half decade, the probers could see the relation of each succeeding murder to the first or key murder of Dean O'Banion in 1924. Until O'Banion was killed there had been some sort of agreement among the bigger men of the bootleg world and Mike Merlo was alive to keep the Sicilians in check, Merlo believing that there was plenty to be made by all and there was no necessity for killings. But Merlo died and before he was buried the Sicilians had eliminated O'Banion from further competition with them and from further hijacking.

Killings on Both Sides

Then followed the shooting of Torrio by Moran, and others, killings on one side and retaliations on the other, the Sicilians "getting" Hymie Weiss and eventually losing their own chieftain, Tony Lombardo, who was slain at Dearborn and Madison street, the center of Chicago's downtown, at 3 o'clock of a summer afternoon.

That slaying indicated an alliance of the powerful Sicilian tribe of the Aiello brothers and the Moran-Gusenberg boys, and the never ending war once more flared up. It sounded simple and logical as veteran detectives pieced the war history together, battle by battle, but it was remarked significantly that "they didn't get Moran or Willie Marks," and it was mentioned that the Aiello brothers have been in seclusion for some time.

Aside from those deductions the officials devoted their time to investigating the Detroit angles. They had confidential sources of information that within the last week several of Detroit's "bad men" were here seeking the names of hijackers who infested the routes from Detroit to Chicago and who "hoisted" the caravans of contraband—confiscated them.

Booze Cargoes Stolen

Word came from Detroit that such a suspicion was well founded. Chicago bound cargoes have been intercepted and stolen, the messages said, and Detroit bootleggers are not known for their gentle dealing with men who rob and despoil them. In the now international code of the rum runners a hijacker is classified as a horse thief formerly was, and a death sentence is always imposed if the hijackers are caught, the officials emphasized.

From some of the Cicero followers of Capone came the suggestion that the financial drain on Moran's purse was so great that he might have plotted their deaths, having them hijack Detroit goods and then betraying them to the Detroiters. The suggestion was given a place in the list of possibilities.

The story of the depressed financial condition of the Moran gang was told, even as the pockets of the dead members were yielding large sums and expensive wrist watches were being taken from the bodies and large diamond rings from the stiffening fingers.

"Body of No. 1," Lieut. John L. Sullivan would announce to Lieut. Otto Erlanson of the homicide bureau, and as it was identified as Pete Gusenberg off came a large diamond ring and $447 in cash. His papers and all were put in a bag.

Gang Hits Hard Times

"Times have been tough for the Moran gang since the gambling joints were put out of business," a squad leader explains. "You see, Moran has to keep a great many men in luxury and money so he'll have them for bodyguards. Formerly he could get them large sums of money by forcing the gambling joints to hire them as inside guards, preventers of stickups.

"The beer racket, which used to be tremendously profitable, has fallen off and all the Moran bunch had to subsist on recently has been the booze and alky business of their boss. Remember the gang trying to kidnap Able Cooper downtown a few months ago. They were desperate to get money and they were unable to operate openly because of the police raids, so they have been sticking up booze and beer cargoes coming here from Detroit. Anything to get a dollar without working. Well, here they are."

Named in Cleaning Racket

"Body No. 2," sings out Lieut. Sullivan, and cards give it the name of Albert Weinshank, and some one asks if it is the former state representative and is told it is his cousin.

Weinshank had only $18 in cash on him when he was killed, but he had a fine diamond ring and a bank book showing his account in the name of A. R. Shanks.

The scene of this grewsome job is in a cleared space in the middle of the long and narrow garage that fronts on Clark street and runs a hundred feet or more west to the alley. Over along the north wall are the bodies. All around are trucks and automobiles.

Back in the rear is a big police dog, chained beneath a truck that Pat Roche of the United States special intelligence service says is a typical beer truck. The dog looks vicious, but he looks scared, too.

They Died Like Dogs

"Seven men died like dogs, but the dog lives," a detective says as he warns others against getting too close to the dog. But the dog does not even bark, he seems mystified that so many strange men dare walk back and forth within his reach.

"Clear the way," order four blue coats, carrying out a stretcher and its burden.

"Body No. 3," Lieut. Sullivan calls to Erlanson, and at first the body is identified as Adam Heyer, who rented the garage, but also as John Snyder, alias Hayes. It is said he was the owner of the Fairview kennels, a dog racing track rivaling Al Capone's Hawthorne dog racing track. "He was the brains of the Moran mob," some one advises Chief Egan.

Heyer had $1,399 in cash in his clothing and the searchers moved over to the next body, that of a man in a brown overall suit, obviously a garage attendant. He later gets the name of John May, an ex-safeblower and the father of seven children. He had but a few dollars in his trousers.

"Look," says Lieut. Erlanson as he takes a leather case from May's back pocket. A machine gun bullet had gone through the case and it had dented two metal objects.

"St. Christopher medals, they are," a policeman reads the inscription. St. Christopher medals are usually carried by motorists, as he is the patron saint of travelers, but sometimes they are given to some one who has led an evil life and whose women relatives think can be reformed if they pray for him and he will pray for himself.

Shotgun Figures in Fusilade

The left part of May's face had been shot off by a shotgun charge. An empty shotgun shell was near by. It was thought he had turned his head around to face the killers just as they fired and the slugs struck his head from the front but the machine gun bullets hit him in the back.

Next to his body was that of the man given the name of Dr. Schwimmer, whom detectives at first thought was Frank Foster. This was the fifth body in a row, all heads to the south and all flat on their backs.

Closer to the wall, face down, head to the east, was the remains of James Clark, brother-in-law of Moran and rated as a killer with many notches in his many guns. His clothes contained $681.

"Four of the bodies have overcoats," the homicide squad notes. "Clark in undercoat only and May in overalls. Count the hats."

Seven Hats are Found

And there were seven hats counted—significant but still no help, as it would be hours, days, or perhaps weeks before the hats could be traced and perhaps they never would be traced to their purchasers.

"Bullet marks on the wall?" Capt. Thomas Condon asks, and it is seen that few of the pellets missed their marks, for there were only seven or eight places where the detectives were sure bullets had struck. Over toward a little bench a saw had been hanging on the wall and the lower part of it had been broken off by a bullet.

The police talk about Mexican firing squads—"the Mexican standoff" they called it—and they expressed amazement that the seven could have been induced to face the wall and certain death without resistance.

"That bunch always went well heeled," a policeman insists, and then Lieut. Loftis states that he has picked up one revolver from the floor—he being the first policeman to arrive—and it had six unfired cartridges.

Woman Tells of Shooting

The explanation was seen in the story of Mrs. Alphonsine Morin, who lives at 2125 North Clark street, just across the street from the garage. She mentioned seeing men she thought were policemen coming out after hearing the shooting.

"Two men in uniforms had rifles or shotguns as they came out the door," she said, "and there were two or three men walking ahead of them with their hands up in the air. It looked as though the police were making an arrest, and they all got into an automobile and drove away."

"Quite simple," Chief Egan comments. "They'd never have got that gang to line up unless they came in police uniforms. They wouldn't have got into the garage unnoticed but it would appear that as policemen they walked in and surprised the gang sitting there and waiting for a message or for orders. For policemen, the gang would line up and face the wall and I suppose the fake policemen disarmed them before they lined them up. Then when the stage was set perhaps the other killers came in and they took aim and started the machine gun and fired the shotguns and then as a precaution against trouble if they should meet policemen coming out, two or three of the killers put up their hands to indicate they were prisoners in custody of police."

Source: *Chicago Daily Tribune*, "Officials Probe Booze Deals in Gang Shooting," February 15, 1929.

The Twenty-first Amendment

The following amendment became part of the United States Constitution on December 5, 1933, repealing the Eighteenth Amendment and ending Prohibition.

Section 1. The eighteenth article of amendment to the Constitution of the United States is hereby repealed.

Section 2. The transportation or importation into any state, territory, or possession of the United States for delivery or use therein of intoxicating liquors, in violation of the laws thereof, is hereby prohibited.

Section 3. This article shall be inoperative unless it shall have been ratified as an amendment to the Constitution by conventions in the several states, as provided in the Constitution, within seven years from the date of the submission hereof to the states by the Congress.

Source: U.S. Constitution, Amendment 21. http://www.archives.gov/national_archives_experience/ charters/constitution_amendments_11-27.html

SOURCES FOR
FURTHER STUDY

Asbury, Herbert. *The Great Illusion: An Informal History of Prohibition*. Garden City, NY: Doubleday & Company, 1950. Traces the evolution of the temperance movement from the colonial era and analyzes the major developments in the enactment and repeal of Prohibition.

Behr, Edward. *Prohibition: Thirteen Years That Changed America*. New York: Arcade Publishing, 1996. Uses bootlegger George Remus as its central focus but also delves into many other aspects of Prohibition, including the corrupt practices of the Harding administration and events in Chicago.

Cashman, Sean Dennis. *Prohibition: The Lie of the Land*. New York: The Free Press, 1981. Concerns itself mostly with events during Prohibition rather than those leading up to it. Extensive coverage of mob activities and the election of 1928.

Coffey, Thomas M. *The Long Thirst: Prohibition in America, 1920-1933*. New York: Norton, 1975. Narrative history that draws together the experiences of more than a dozen of the most important figures of the Prohibition era.

Kobler, John. *Ardent Spirits: The Rise and Fall of Prohibition*. New York: G. P. Putnam's Sons, 1973. Entertaining and authoritative account that covers alcohol's role in American history, the fight to enact Prohibition, and events during the 1920s and early 1930s.

Mason, Philip P. *Rumrunning and the Roaring Twenties: Prohibition on the Michigan-Ontario Waterway*. Detroit, MI: Wayne State University Press, 1995. A treasure trove of historical photos accompanied by an interesting overview of bootlegging activities in the Detroit-Windsor area.

Sinclair, Andrew. *Prohibition: The Era of Excess*. Boston: Little, Brown, 1962. In-depth analysis of the social and psychological elements underlying Prohibition.

BIBLIOGRAPHY

Books and Periodicals

Adams, John. *Diary and Autobiography*. Cambridge: Harvard University Press, 1961.

Addams, Jane. "Prohibition and Chicago." *Survey Graphic*, October 1929.

Albini, Joseph L. *The American Mafia: Genesis of a Legend*. New York: Appleton-Century-Crofts, 1971.

Allen, Frederick Lewis. *Only Yesterday: An Informal History of the 1920s*. New York: Harper & Brothers, 1931.

Anderson, Paul Y. "The Inside Story of the Amazing Career of George Remus, Multimillionaire Bootlegger and His Band of Rumrunners." *St. Louis Post-Dispatch*, January 3-20, 1926.

Asbury, Herbert. *The Great Illusion: An Informal History of Prohibition*. Garden City, NY: Doubleday & Company, 1950.

Baughman, Judith S., ed. *American Decades: 1920-1929*. Detroit, MI: Gale Research, 1996.

Behr, Edward. *Prohibition: Thirteen Years That Changed America*. New York: Arcade Publishing, 1996.

Bruére, Martha. *Does Prohibition Work?* New York: Harper & Brothers, 1927.

Cashman, Sean Dennis. *Prohibition: The Lie of the Land*. New York: The Free Press, 1981.

Chidsey, Donald Barr. *On and Off the Wagon: A Sober Analysis of the Temperance Movement from the Pilgrims through Prohibition*. New York: Cowles Book Co., 1969.

Coffey, Thomas M. *The Long Thirst: Prohibition in America, 1920-1933*. New York: Norton, 1975.

Dabney, Virginius. *Dry Messiah: The Life of Bishop Cannon*. New York: Alfred A. Knopf, 1949.

Einstein, Izzy. *Prohibition Agent No. 1*. New York: Frederick A. Stokes, 1932.

Enforcement of the Prohibition Laws: Official Records of the National Commission on Law Observance and Enforcement. 5 vols. Washington, D.C.: U.S. Government Printing Office, 1931.

Finan, Christopher M. *Alfred E. Smith: The Happy Warrior*. New York: Hill and Wang, 2002.

Gosch, Martin A., and Richard Hammer. *The Last Testament of Lucky Luciano*. Boston: Little, Brown, 1974.

Hall, Bolton. *Thrift*. New York: B. W. Huebsch, 1916.

Haynes, Roy A. *Prohibition Inside Out*. Garden City, NY: Doubleday, Page & Company, 1923.

Kobler, John. *Ardent Spirits: The Rise and Fall of Prohibition.* New York: G. P. Putnam's Sons, 1973.

Kobler, John. *Capone: The Life and World of Al Capone.* New York: G. P. Putnam's Sons, 1971.

Labaree, Benjamin W., et al. *America and the Sea: A Maritime History.* Mystic, CT: Mystic Seaport Museum, 1998.

Lippmann, Walter. "The Great Wickersham Mystery." *Vanity Fair,* April 1931.

Lippmann, Walter. "Our Predicament under the Eighteenth Amendment." *Harper's Magazine,* December 1926.

Mason, Philip P. *Rumrunning and the Roaring Twenties: Prohibition on the Michigan-Ontario Waterway.* Detroit, MI: Wayne State University Press, 1995.

McLoughlin, William G., Jr. *Billy Sunday Was His Real Name.* Chicago: University of Chicago Press, 1955.

Merz, Charles. *The Dry Decade.* Garden City, NY: Doubleday, Doran, 1931.

Pegram, Thomas R. *Battling Demon Rum: The Struggle for a Dry America, 1800-1933.* Chicago: Ivan R. Dee, 1998.

Repetto, Thomas. *American Mafia: A History of Its Rise to Power.* New York: Henry Holt and Company, 2004.

Rogers, Will. *The Cowboy Philosopher on Prohibition.* New York: Harper & Brothers, 1919.

Roosevelt, Franklin D. *The Public Papers and Addresses of Franklin D. Roosevelt.* Vol. 1, *The Genesis of the New Deal 1928-1932.* New York: Random House, 1938.

Rush, Benjamin. *An Inquiry into the Effects of Spirituous Liquors on the Human Body: To Which is Added, a Moral and Physical Thermometer.* Boston: Thomas and Andrews, 1790.

Sinclair, Andrew. *Prohibition: The Era of Excess.* Boston: Little, Brown, 1962.

Steuart, Justin. *Wayne Wheeler: Dry Boss.* New York: Fleming H. Revell Company, 1928.

Terkel, Studs. *Hard Times: An Oral History of the Great Depression.* New York: Pantheon Books, 1970.

Van de Water, Frederic F. *The Real McCoy.* Garden City, NY: Doubleday, Doran & Company, 1931.

Veblen, Thorstein. *The Theory of the Leisure Class.* New York: Modern Library, 1934.

Wendt, Lloyd, and Herbert Kogan. *Big Bill of Chicago.* Indianapolis: Bobs-Merrill, 1953.

Willebrandt, Mabel Walker. *The Inside of Prohibition.* Indianapolis: The Bobbs-Merrill Company, 1929.

Online

Cato Institute. "Alcohol Prohibition was a Failure." http://www.cato.org/pubs/pas/pa-157.html

Ohio State University Department of History. "Temperance & Prohibition." http://prohibition.history.ohio-state.edu

Prohibition Party. Official web site. http://www.prohibition.org

DVD and VHS

The Prohibition Era. 3 vols. DVD. A&E Home Video, 1997.

PHOTO CREDITS

INDEX